CW01650667

Diamonds In Streams

Selected Poems Vol. 3

Steve Day

Grosvenor House
Publishing Limited

This book is published by
Grosvenor House Publishing Ltd
Link House
140 The Broadway, Tolworth, Surrey, KT6 7HT.
www.grosvenorhousepublishing.co.uk

A CIP record for this book
is available from the British Library

ISBN 978-1-83975-850-8

Cover credits:
Jon Ogborne, graphics (Eat Cake Design)
Stacey Burling, front cover photograph
Alex Wilson, back cover photograph

Picture credits:
Jon Ogborne, *The Frome*, photograph
Mary Griese, *Handsome Boy*, painting
Sergio Armaroli, *Dance Steps*, Design
Jon Ogborne, *Country Road 2020*, photograph
Unknown Artist, *The Blue Horn*, graffiti Palma

Previous Work By Steve Day

Poetry
Day By Day (South West Arts)
The Edge Of England: Selected Poems Vol.1 (Grosvenor House Pub.)
Curving Sentences: Selected Poems Vol. 2 (Grosvenor House Pub.)
Pairing (FreeTone Records)

Prose
Two Full Ears: Listening to improvised music (Soundworld)
Ornette Coleman: Music Always (Soundworld)
Free Jazz - chapter from Masters Of Jazz Saxophone (Backbeat/Freeman Miller)
Looks Like Leisure? - chapter (with Nick Fripp)
from Intellectual Disability & Social Inclusion (Churchill Livingstone)
The Ganelin Trio – A Russian Triptych (Palmyra Pub.)

Music
Visitors (Leo Records)
Song Of The Fly (Leo Records)
Strewn With Pebbles (Leo Records)

As a member of Blazing Flame:
Blazing Flame Play High Mountain Top (Leo Records)
Blazing Flame: Murmuration (Leo Records)
Blazing Flame Quintet: The Set List Shuffle (Leo Records)
Blazing Flame Quintet/6: Wrecked Chateau (Leo Records)

Publications include reviews, articles & poetry for *What's New* (Sandy Brown Jazz), *Avant, Eureka, Serious* & others;
liner notes for labels such as *Leo Records*, *FMP* & *Splasch.*

Diamonds In Streams, Selected Poems Vol. 3: dedicated
to the great poet Federico García Lorca (1898 - 1936)

*"Steve, you honoured Lorca. Integrity runs through
all of your poems... full of care and insight."*
Phil Madden, *Poet*

Thank you to:
Megan Day & Stacey Burling, Bryony & Arya Burgess,
Doug & Kerry Day, Jon & Liz Ogborne, Julian Dale, Peter Evans,
Michael & Elaine Gibson, Bingo Fury, Mary Griese, Alex Wilson,
James Stallard, Mark Langford, Pete Brownlee, Bill Bartlett,
Julie Tippetts, Sergio Armaroli, Leo Feigin, Ian Maund, Phil Madden,
Andy Williamson, Martin Walsh & Harriet Tamlin, Clive Dawson &
Gloria Burland, Sam Forster, Tom Wilding, Alex & Lynne Easton,
Jennie Osborne, Becky Banning.

*"Nothing that concerns us, in our brief moment of history,
gives us the right to stop time, to blot out the future, to end the
continuing miracles and glories and tragedies
and wretchedness of the human race."*
Martha Gellhorn, *The Face Of War*

*"It occurred to me, as the heavy curtains were opened
and the morning light flooded the small dining area,
that without doubt we sometimes eclipse
our own dreams with reality."*
Patti Smith, *M Train*

Contents

Diamonds In Streams

March 2019 - April 2020

Preface

Diamonds In Streams is about the content of living. The trove of every day treasure. It's aligned to what historian Mary Beard called the *Eye Of Faith*. She eschews theorising religion, as do I. Faith, simply seeing spark and sparkle in the world around us. My well seasoned friend and confidant Jon Ogborne spends a lot of time in rivers and streams. He tells me he goes fishing. What I observe is Jon's mind collecting diamonds.

The light translucent, mirroring nature in wild water. *Diamonds In Streams* is a fraction of my writings between March 2019 to September 2021. In my few 'live' readings during this period nearly all the poems were taken from the post-May 2020 section of this collection. They are among the most accurate and acute poetry I've written. We all know diamonds come with a cost, often found in the darkest places. Diamonds carry a price tag. In my book, a mix of fact, faith and ownership, "all damming the same stream."

Steve Day

Diamonds In Streams

May 2020 - September 2021

The Light From Diamonds In Streams

Chaucer might have met them. The Miners
for immortal diamonds, not only theirs
but one for everybody else too.
Like hidden treasures in the temporal lobe
they inexplicitly discover Marilyn warbling:
Diamonds are a girl's best friend.
Strange how Rohr believed he was quoting
Hopkins searching for his eternal soul.

Another Eldorado where they know eternity
finds immortality sparkling in cut glass.
Forever will eventually fade into
us all damming the same stream. The trout
in the shallows, early curling fern, the light
from diamonds in streams now a
road across the hills, fenced and tree lined,
a simple journey not a holy pilgrimage.

A Franciscan friar lit an altar candle though
he always knew birth is to be preferable
to death and even for a man of
his persuasion the final breath scared him.
Like the rest of us, the other side is secret.
But here's the thing of it, we see
meaning in the passing of flowing waters.
No need to hold life merely touch it.

For Richard Rohr

Stacey's Photograph

Stacey's photograph of figures
in a landscape has Megan wearing
Bryony's boots; we had decided to stroll
beside the river, beside the point, watch
the sun play out in the torrent of the current.
Hear birdsong's flute sing to every tree,
plant a place of safety against the rushing
order of things. We can walk the day away.

From her beginning she has always glided
across grass. Knowing such a journey's end
even when the pattern drawn in black and white
comes not in the most obvious order. This was a
description of her clothing at the Absolute's bend
in the river, with water as see-through as the soul
and it fitted the afternoon's pale blue blessed sky
as if told whole she'd dressed to contrast the fiesta
crest of Bright Phoebus above the cumulus clouds.

He, strolling with half an ear to hear what is
so clear to everyone by now.
Megan is a woman in touch with herself,
able to catch the light of day without attachment.
Two figures wander into a Georges Seurat painting,
then amble out the other side. An array of wisdom
from a moorland's riverbank more crucial
than a sideshow circus.

Prometheus

Dispense with the gender description.
Narrow to the life, the level of the eye
line, voice modulating like well-tuned
drums. The faint film of paint stroked
across the scent of soap. They are the
rib cage and its beating heart. Muscle
detached from
the skeletal string of skinny veins
threaded through an exposed arm pit.
Lean lettering speaking science
as a giant of humanity.
Last Will and Testament
in the manner of a monk
by the river setting alight
the family funeral pyre.

This is where we meet Prometheus,
paddling a skiff for hire.
We barter for the boat to take us
across to the far side of our fiction.
A place born out of the body of ribs and
dissonance. Dance dalliance
on this white water of
rocks and plotted currents surging
towards a sea of stars in
the night sky. Who
is such a figure of silence? Who calls
the name Prometheus?

He be the waterboatwoman, a liver
of emotion gives away a
god of florescent-flame becoming
a child on a river wide as the ocean.
Prometheus rows with a body as bellows.
Piston arms, legs of titanium,
fire in the binary belly.
The hair shirt icon who once ferried
plutonium now explains
the terms of travel:
"I charge no fee yet no one will cross
such a river for free."

The Vibe In Yellow Roses

This year they carried on blooming
as if yellow roses cannot cease putting
out petals to remind us
what you already know.
The vibe is in the earth.
Composted into the fiber
of the very ground we grow in.
Every sentient being contributes a death
to the texture of soiling the body
back into the land beneath us.
Weary be the final breath,
but bud on stem, bud on stem, then
at the end a flowering of yellow roses.

For E & M

Ram With Horns

She painted a ram with horns
that looked like rhino
and called it Handsome Boy.
I cannot say that I could wrestle
him to the floor to shear the fleece
from the pale skin nor taste the lanolin
of his coat or even whistle to drive
dogs to bring such a beast to order.
Animals as this are pure border country
and I know not the bounds
of the parish and cannot claim his name
for myself, a ram with horns curled
backwards with bravado.

Whatever I now have left over is
not in this painting of a
male sheep with eyes alight to
darkness but for sure I have arable
seed and could sow fields with wheat.
Not so that it would cut bread but I write
good words, at least good enough to
keep the dead dead and the living in a
far country populated with the survival of
kindness and the end of Eden.
Handsome Boy with horns is a picture to
conjure with; one to take home and
put on the precious shelf.

For slightly sheepish M

Slow Worm

No snake in the grass,
Slow Worm
the legless lizard
                    is a circle of suspense
laying motionless beneath the flax.
An afternoon bleached in heat, we eating
a warm salad of sundried tomato, a mind's
eye fixed on the curled reptile.
Detailed scale by scale in body-part.
No one wants to move.

Thick Skin

A close poetic shave;
the Church and the Birch rhyme.
Everyone who has got near to him
has seen the sacred sign
upon his backbone.
Dry chaffed sore, wearing a desert
has him fly-tipping his pores,
rubbing his flakey body creamed
to the meat of the male.
Rough in sleep and recognition,
his right hand continually gloved
his left always sprayed clean.

What he holds is Leviticus,
the guts of the Torah
in sanctimonious sacrifice.
A convert in the convent cloisters
stripped to a loin cloth like the
paintings of their Lord and Master.
No need to give King Lear away.
Maybe that was his purpose in
coming here, to lose a layer
and keep his eyes shut tight.

Now all bets are off,
even a man as thinly clothed as he
is well versed in the possession
of shadow around his shaven jaw-line.
And if he has written tragedy into a corner,
so be it, let him lick the envelope too.
The title deeds are not lost, neither are
they found by any extravagant display
of saving his own stubble.
It matters not what
old men remember.
The thicker their skin
the thinner their memory.

Peregrine

A year after my world went silent as a stone
I took a terraced house in the lower town facing
out towards the busy road, the quarry and a pair
of peregrine nesting on a crevice ledge.
Perhaps that's what I'm doing too.
It feels like I can white streak
creases into the view.

I watch these two birds flying their shape
of eight as if leaving vapor trails patterned into
place. And I acknowledge them as neighbours in
the sky circling across Blue Elvan stone.
I took a house in this terraced row
and the peregrine returned
all I need to know.

A Recognisable Specimen

Angled poised lamp, switched off.
Through the tied back curtain
sharp sun strikes the glass.
The coding shutter's click produces
art pictures unmasked with insight
thrown onto the subject.
In my view a closed opening
published for your attention.

These pages are written in a vaccine.
Protection against getting ahead of myself.
Detailed portrait of a recognisable specimen.
The results speak for themselves in the vein
of a noted author of improvising techniques.
I puncture the paper with the pressure
of a camera's direct hit on a full-stop.

Carefully, with deliberation tear-up
the original attempt at daylight and in the
process, shredding light on what awaits me.
Now I unload the ballpoint behind a redrawn
curtain. Wait for this photo shoot to provide
proofs of a week's worth of riddles via
visual evidence from the camera lens.

For the writer and photographer Alex Wilson.

So Am I

I am out. So am I.
And there we are in two other worlds.
It is implausible, impossible, to constantly
inhabit the same territory in every hour
and therefore we sometimes write:
I am out. So am I.
Be happy for each other that there is
a continuum to attend to.
Then when we coalesce
maybe we will dance together
or if it is not to be a dancing day
perhaps we will read aloud and enjoy
the tone and tremor of the reader
contemplating the preface.
Embrace the vocal modulation and emphasis
as in the floor-craft on an uneven unlit ballroom.
Heel to toe, and swirl and go, twist, turn
toward the door ajar.
I am in. So am I.

Reprise

(i)

This isn't a hobby, writing suites of strings
into tension to curve a cello wood
detuned of any breath and oxygen.
This isn't a neon Saturday night love affair
keeping a bow's distance from each
other when we have stories to share.
This is the reason to sing the second string
because it's carried as a composition
and in five verses, all that I can bring.
Play Stravinsky as if this is his first time out
sitting in the virgin audience of ears
straining hard to hear a cello count.

(ii)

Weaving through a rooted woodland held in
abeyance as the eyes plot the routes of ants
repairing their tiny holes in the bank.
Observations like these are not going
to be a second verse attempting to
make the best of it.
I came here to live again, to collect
leaves, watch them curl into a curtsy
as they age and in their brittle bending
split apart from the tree.
This friendship is not different from
something else because something else
passed by but here among the moss
and loam smells the scent
of every colony we call coming home.

(iii)

Third time lucky is an unattractive
proposition for which there is
no interest and no percentage charged.
I'll not scratch out one line of the past
or attempt to rewrite it for the future.

(iv)

Now on a fourth trip to the holy land
where sleep abides with me
in the mycelium. A spirit walks on
the Dart without any argument,
waving wind from a litter of stars
speckling the repetitive rushing water.
Death talk in hemlock, resurrection fungi,
bees make honey in the hive box and the
Nazarene throws stones into the current.

(v)

This isn't a hobby, writing suites of strings
weaving through a rooted woodland held in
proposition for which there is
the Dart without any argument.
And the sound of water slips away
in the rain puddling the path into river.

For my friend Julian Dale
based on his 2nd Suite For Strings.

Slowly As With The Hour

Sleep folded away in unironed sheets
slowly as with the hour peaking through
the window collecting our morning and
singling a precious stone.
In April he takes his old Skoda packing.
We meet, condense chapter and verse in
a jewellery box; squint eyes shape the
views of adopted moorland.

Surely he would recognise a diamond
among the glass baubles kept as tokens
to Buddha. Later both of us are able to
confirm its authenticity.
There is colossal permanence in learnt
practices of giving up a personal wealth.
One of us found the sound of the bass
the other, an article of faith.

Neither easy on the ear, lost for words,
entwined in a double bass-line of letters.
So explicit in simplicity. He plucks each
arpeggio with a sense of arco.
When we meet again in October I have
gained the perfect portrait of a horned
ram's head. Each eye follows my eyes
blurred by bright diamonds.

Buckland Beacon

We had strolled here from the road
I mesmerised by the view of the far distance.
An escaped landscape caught
in shadow and light, my companion
describing Princetown and incarceration.
As she did so it was as if we moved through
the fair imagining her mother
playing the piano by ear.
An agitated skylark hung above us, too
near its nest. The bird dropping like a stone
to the ground once we'd kept our distance.

And it was easy for me to pick my path
onto Buckland Beacon, the ever present
vertigo not kicking in. I stood still for a
moment, lord of all I beheld. We owned
no one nor the thought of it.
Someone has decided to carve the Ten
Commandments into stone, reminding
us not to murder. At this point, way out
of reach of us they have declared
a ceasefire, but hell's teeth when will we
call it peace? So far yet so near to beauty.

Wet Reeds For A Queen's Swarm

Beyond Bonehill Rocks and Hound Tor,
a green tweed path between loose stone
to Teignmouth estuary.
A long way from Wales
even further Donegal.
Stretch horizon's mizzle memory
to faraway Fishguard and the Irish ferry.

Sitting on sheep droppings
humming rough passages of hymnal.
A man, head high in raincloud and a
dry stone refuge, parts a stained
curtain of Whitlow grass to count
his sheep bleating for their salvation.

This was my first sight of Niall,
alive as you are me; waged him my
sin for his and bought myself more
time navigating the old way lamb line
from here on an escarpment to a tree
planted by Joseph in the myth of it.
But he is real enough, washing clean
hands in a can of muddy water.

Niall, bearded naturalist of rock
face, cutting reed for bee hives,
twisting mist to store a dome in
warm straw provides
honey for mead.

So says the recipe, the spell book
of his magic: *"The only word I put
to paper is a whisper and that is
now not worth a birth certificate."*
He says the sentence as if it were
a law of average covered in thorn
and briar. Later, Niall said:
"Once upon a time I murdered a man."

Such stories go as they go, painfully
slow, full of pause, creaking in
confession turning out thirty years.
He had shot dead a Derry brother
because he had hurt a child.

The truth in troublin' times; it took
away his soul to a prison block and
left it there, on ice, to feel the cold.
Pitted grime grit shit smeared thick
across the scarred brick walls. Note
of knowledge, a dead sheep worn by
a shepherd. Later, Niall said:
"A man gives nothing up but *his soul."*

And so it is that I remember him, alive
as I am you, skilfully working wet
reeds for a Queen's swarm. Seeking
what cannot be seen, the old bridleway

trekked between the trig point and
Princetown. A man of no abode with
a past left carved in stone in County
Mayo sat mapping my new home.
I stand alone on the ridge line
surveying belief. I cannot fall, after
all, this is moor not mountain.
Men give nothing up but their soul.

Lorca

Lorca ran into her before the war
had finally settled on Spain.
He apologised. This would not be
the last time he had cause to do so.
Perhaps the first occasion is always the worse
because a woman still has yet to discover
how much monster is left in the mistaken mask.

Lorca is not that way inclined, for
he rides a black pony and
cannot reach Cordova. He has to
scribble his days in the dust of the
night, a man with Walt Whitman in his pocket.
A heart of chalk; love comes written white
cleaning his path with a bouquet of peace lilies.

Federico García was not a man to
carry his apology lightly.
A penance to all women becomes
the tested justification to everyman.
In the same way as Andalusia must be Granada
poetry is an Appaloosa stallion that cannot
be ridden without this handmade leather saddle.

Hepworth

Hepworth left London for St Ives.
As did I.
The same narrow road south to see
a garden of sculptured monoliths.
I often found Hepworth
when not looking for her hands
pressing polished pitted marble.

This was but one of her holy moments,
the dismembering of the thin silk veil.
Too tatty no one else ever seemed to notice.
Now there is nobody to talk to her about shape
nor the perfect position of gaping holes.
Hepworth's blunt thumb vigorously
rubbing at the blemished surfaces.

A storm of stones thrown with all the tenacity
of great art at a granite banquet.
Everybody loved her, I know.
Today no one is allowed to come that close.
Not enough to understand how she inwardly
moans for a meagre supper of stones
to be slowly digested on their own.
The idea of such a simple meal is denied her.

On fish-scale nights when the sky greys
with a sense of breezing fever the stars
glance eye to earth and earth to a mass
of endless universe.
Eternity an orgasm, bright momentary
awakening and then the glint
of a new moon through a bronze eye.

Below Trewyn,
Hepworth and Ben Nicholson
walking the bay across
seagrass and rock pools before high tide.
I imagine them and remember that day
and what it meant to leave it all behind.

There is no companion to scent her bath
with seaweed and samphire.
Now no one strolls with Hepworth, whispering
for the long eared hare to hear and rise to run.
Her fading eyesight notices not the thin silk veil
and so fails to carefully tie it tight to her waist.
They who once guarded her life are soiled.
Only afterwards am I aware fingers have dared
to touch Hepworth's cast metal with verdigris.
No matter, for she
has sculptured a space free of their solidity.

Dedicated to Barbara Hepworth, sculptor and artist.
(10th January 1903 - 20th May 1975)

Doug

Two Day's apart make
amends more thorough
than any season spent nurturing
an allotment of roots and greens.
Doug out of the grass
a spades length to his name.
Digging for salvation already
won a long time ago.
The word of earth and peat
composed from Essex clay
on Sinai's Westcliff.
There, buried under the sediment
is our own body of evidence
perfectly preserved.

My dear brother, the one of us who held
onto the harvest and simply opened all
his goodwill and faith into our affection.
Of all the boys back then he
was the best of them and he
Doug himself out of the earth
with the firm conviction of
a true believer.

There was a time when we missed each
other's footprints. Even then I knew he
held on to himself while I was blowing
in the hurricane. Oh yes, I worshipped
the angel and Doug possessed no one,
yet found someone and in
that narrow way there was
room for two.

No matter what was done in
the past, it remains where it lays
Doug beyond our depth of belief.
Soil breached beneath the maze
of microbes budding leaf to leaf.
Two Day's today, his love for me
and mine for him.

Truly he is the resurrection
and the life, my kin.
I am his blooded brother.
I can never desert him or deserve
him, nor lose Doug from my mind.

Tidy Man

He had tidied away his life;
privacy-word-perfect.
It didn't run smoothly out
of his ears in waves of emotion.
He kept it under wraps to himself
like a secret discipline.
It wasn't there for public display;
merely to be contained
in the bathroom cabinet to be
taken out only when required.

His indulgencies could be
about every grain of
gravel on the carpet, how
clean are the soles of slippers?
He would give as much as he could
but he would not share
it, not that part, intimacies are an
investment, what he picked
up from the street was between
himself and the black bin liner.

She to him, his to her and
time to both of them.
Neither uttered any word
of evidence to implicate bird
or beast. If he swept every corner
he could be sure there
was still more to do in the centre
of the room. Go let them eat
sand and shit mountains. He is
a tidy man, that's the end of it.

Weather Box

For months she came to my rescue for one night per week. Over this kitchen table we travelled to places we had never visited for more than a moment. The old country new to us both.

During these evenings I am unafraid. She is so sure, the facts of it feel as rich a pasture as I have ever witnessed. I hear her describe the past not as an affirmation. All the rough edges are

tough stuff not papered over yet neither do we miss out the Weather Box or the tandem ride along the canal to the tea garden where the cakes rose like castles. The ingredient is spiced sugar.

Now that we know that things will always be acknowledged between us. Here in this sold kitchen, over the laden table, we travelled to a love of understanding each other that has consequence.

Household bubbles burst; I never heard the
warning hiss, I missed the moment. But she
is the wise watchwoman, able to blow fresh
air into her own climate and delineate wind
from storms.

For dearest B
"It's the past that tells us who we are. Without it we lose our identity."
Stephen Hawking.

Tolstoy Beneath The Beard

Tolstoy told tall tales
so much bigger than I
my mind so much man to the master
far too low from the sky.
To name a star would be like
attempting to call Shostakovich a tune
when my ears hear only symphony.

Tolstoy had laid down
weapons before Russia
had entered the war, later a polite
English guy enquired why
Stalingrad had been renamed
after a saint and the light of the world
exploded by an American bomb.

Tolstoy is beneath the
beard, a scarf he didn't
have to pay for, he kept it on in all
weathers. To the naked eye
he was a picture of Russia. As
a writer his pen wrote every piece for
every nation as a peace to them.

Hercules

They said he was a tough little
bugger who could be relied upon
to make it through until Mecca.
People throw out such erroneous
comments when they don't like
risking travelling such a perilous
journey. We can't all be Hercules.

Such a mighty man as this who
has travelled seven seas now falls
to the floor like an old sailor of
survival. Every day he must try to
fish in the stream, net enough
to feed fortune twenty four bright
hours of daylight for safe keeping.

The saving grace of Hercules is
his ability to believe in beauty as
the epitome of compassion and
find it in himself for himself. With
a withered arm lacking any grip,
his decaying hand holds not only
a slip of paper but the final word.

A Report From Lashkargāh

Now reporting from a front line
which until the captured tank rolled in
that morning had been the vegetable market
south of the city. She describes the speed
of the advance into chaos, how quickly it comes.

The hotel is nothing more than
a room of worn walls under mortar fire.
The unmade bed not an exhibition statement
just a fucking mattress, sheets aired for
the afternoon to give them some breathing space.

No, there has been insufficient
time to verify exactly who is among the
dead, most of them are civilians. Yes children
of course, the school is at the crossroads,
they were gathering for lessons when it happened.

Can she describe the slaughter?
No, you do not need to hear the graphic
detail of death you have heard it a hundred times
before. It is as it always will be forever more.
Today with us, but you too will recognise it I'm sure.

DANCE STEPS
for Sergio Armaroli & Roger Turner

Two step duet,
rub a balance & code prepared vibes
sourcing a space in-between maps of
traps in each other's choreography.
Blank verse where no words matter
amongst the clatter of tap & tangle.
A tiny tease skims the rim of rumba
symbolising cymbals of dancing bars.
Hurt-not-the-hitters, hit not to hurt
an Armaroli Turner display splaying
faint fractures of ballroom street music.
Jolt… a light touch fingering felt heads
carrying hammered intimacy, cavorting
silence to a shimmering palladium
of Paste Duchamp objet d'art.
A loose rolling rattle holds
this two step percussive pirouette
a plague distance from the precise
pause of prima ballerina. & on number
nine: one two three 4 one two three 4
heel & flow one two freely.
Cascade a way through the flip of stick
to mallet in a circle of ping & flats.
Two dancers reeling into plats of woven
coalescence, obviously beating but not
beaten, duet but not dual. An instant
cluster of compositions play deference to
dance entranced by tip-toe, tip-toe, toe-tip.

Steve Day, *2021*

Dance Steps

Two step duet,
rub a balance & code prepared vibes
sourcing a space in-between maps of
traps in each other's choreography.
Blank verse where no words matter
amongst the clatter of tap & tangle.
A tiny tease skims the rim of rumba
symbolising cymbals of dancing bars.
Hurt-not-the-hitters, hit not to hurt
an Armaroli Turner display splaying
faint fractures of ballroom street music.
Jolt... a light touch fingering felt heads
carrying hammered intimacy, cavorting
silence to a shimmering palladium
of Paste Duchamp objet d'art.
A loose rolling rattle holds
this two step percussive pirouette
a plague distance from the precise
pause of prima ballerina. & on number
nine: one two three 4 one two three 4
heel & flow one two *freely*.
Cascade a way through the flip of stick
to mallet in a circle of ping & flats.
Two dancers reeling into plats of woven
coalescence, obviously beating but not
beaten, duet but not dual. An instant
cluster of compositions play deference to
dance entranced by tip-toe, tip-toe, toe-tip.

For Sergio Armaroli & Roger Turner

Ode To Charlie Haden

Charlie Haden played double bass
like an astronaut in a checked shirt and tie.
He continually took bottom to the top giving
ground to gravity,
closing the circumference
of poor people's lives whilst circling the skies.
A notated
passage
walking
the zigzag
line
through to liberation.
Orchestrating voices of the Fallen. Soloist in the
timbre and the varnish patina on the tree of life.
A blues beneath the cry of Morrison's *Bluest Eye*.
The sonic pulse of whales encrypted by the bow.
Ornette's violin scratching at this *Science Fiction*.
An abuser's regime: "I accuse it of a lack of love."
Charlie plays for all prisoners of conscience who
gather to sing *Feliciano Ama* - the dawn will set
itself afire in El Salvador.

Officials invent rules about inflammatory politics
and the art of playing an antique bass; check the
face on the passport to make sure Senhor Haden
gets to grace a night in a rat biting prison for his
Song For Che. The Portuguese DGS return him to
America and the FBI say tango is a dance of spies.

His doubling bass, squares the rhythmic density, popping free modulation, carrying the big fiddle every station of the cross counting up the times a chorus is lost. The seeker projects the twist of dissonance and folk song. "I fill a space, only if I am asked to. Ornette and I, we orbit our melody."

For All My Mothers And Fathers

"Certainty, we neither know it nor need it."
Evading a mouth full of questions without
answers. His father a silent sculpture; his
linguistics are heard in a collapsible river.

A deconstructing waterfall pours through
a sieve collecting the phlegm of lipsticks.
Sighting such words drawn into the walls
are strips of scratched bat shit in Sanskrit.

The gender does not come as a surprise.
Her captors try to tease such things away.
Michelangelo's marble, touch stone Pietà,
make her a mother and feel her hot heart.

Each chip, chip at emotion is denied daily.
Eve was blamed by priests from the start.
Visible and bloody the sacrificial calf left
on the bank of the river to decay unclean.

She dances in red threads of chiffon and
for one final time the corps de ballet leap
and twirl over an audience of refugees as
if they are scattering stone across a road.

This inadequate description of humanity
cannot disguise the fact everyone is now
named Eve. Uncertainty becomes an edge
of Eden and another name for possibility.

For all my mothers and fathers, every one
of them, the line of their travel is the line
I read to you. Our parents are thousands
in the great mixture of multiple ethnicity.

Their lives planted out across this planet
in a family tree with roots as deep as the
sleep of progeny. We are all in migration
and a deconstructed waterfall of dynasty.

Because Of It

Under a sagging telephone
wire was where a has been
handsome old-hat sat to sip
his wounds through teeth unable
to prevent him bursting into his
refrains to the damn audience
of one, despite the pain or
because of it.

Another beaten up bygone
balladeer, too deaf to hear
his tolling bell rung wrong.
Flat as a pierced lung struck by
the weighted gong which keeps
time ticking yet gives an echo
he couldn't quite get near
because of it.

Even from a distance it was
possible to count out each
chord in the rhythm of life.
Those changes regularly barred
hitting the beats of his wayward
heart every time a faint sound
of song carried hallelujah
because of it.

He is not the thief stealing
underneath a life to own a
voice that sings so sweet.
If this be how the past is played
then bygones be truly hiding in
those old songs still offering
their softly sung melodies
because of it.

Leitmotif

The tears in the morning, the
dark *mourning* heart
bereft of a new day from which to
start again.
She rains her sorrow as first light
catches the
horizon, a chorus comes into land,
            a chorale flock of birds in
mourning for the crumbs of an old
man sprinkling his ashes.

Take out those morning tears in the
weeping showers before the sun can
rise, dawn will paint another surprise
promise bending with the mourning
for her dead further-along father.
Come the anthem of birds
singing for a dark *morning* heart
masquerading at his funeral wake.

Blue Kali, White Man

He barely looked old enough
to inhabit a face of his own
though the cavernous brittle lines
grew deeper by the end of day
her perception was the rough
clay of a philosopher's stone,
chipped away by the sands of time,
said more than his wordplay.

Who could ever expect a man
to pardon himself overnight?
Shakti blurs his eyesight of memory
and recognition of awakening.
How can he try to understand
her desire to hold him tight?
Whatever passes is but a temporary
hallucination slowly breaking.

His hands are an unread map
of valleys and veins. He has
gripped the same card trick taught
him as a child; found an Ace
rises to the top of the pack.
An arrowhead A, always as
Kali, deeper than dark blue, caught
in a rendezvous with grace.

Lent Lotus

He enters a fading sepia childhood
surrounded by the satanic mills of
Jerusalem, a memorised modernity.
Sing out Sunday to Charles Wesley
a harmonised herd of frogs mating
in the wings of the polluted pond.
No one wants to tell teacher about
a fat blotchy butcher who cuddled

kids on the split-back-seats of the
bus, his itchy sticky fingers prying
into the Lord's Prayer to touch the
mass of boyhood ever so squidgy
yet too hard to feel. A terrible tale,
just when we are watching Petula
Clark on the television glowing in
the dark. Our newly mown garden

has scarlet roses but scarlet roses
have thorns and every septic prick
is treated with a lemon's poultice.
Decades later a Lent lotus begins
to open Blake and Buddha's eyes.
Suburbia surprised; menstruation
is mentioned in the Bible and the
poor relations found blood at My

Lai massacre, the same terror as at Omaha Beach. Siddhartha was not crucified on a cross, instead caught napping beneath the tree at Bodh Gaya. The lotus floats in amongst the weed and the frogs croak like kings crowned for the ceremonial sake of staying quiet.

Drum – for Dom Um Romão

To do what they said they would
do, do do.
But don't, don't, don't, can't, can't, can't.
That is the way of it until the big hit
bounces once on the bass skin, twice on the shell,
overhear Romão tell a quick grip rhythm
to tongue and groove repetition going
can, can, can, must, must, must
find a-finer point to
beat, beat, beat it up by playing stick fingers
from the wrist by hand drum.
Rub the thumb
torrent of touch and
go, go, go:
throb of godhead struck on nail tip and knuckle,
palm handling centre skin rim and the weight
of the heavy hand.
The right like a fated blurred percussion prayer
against the light left
adding interjecting talking drum to itself.

Come Sunday gospel thunder clap.
Come Monday take it back.
Come Tuesday spread layers of beats
to keep a whole week working toward Friday
and the Saturday samba sex pummelled out in
four, four, four - four
in an endless roll of index finger lick tricks
playing space and motion
into *Boogie Woogie Waltz*.

Şakici

A woman with two lives lives beside
two rivers.
You understand?
This is a voice deliberately leaking life
bordering the intensity and necessity
of song inscribed by fire.
Yet there is no name on the billboard
nor flame ignited.
But all rivers flow to one almighty ocean.

She sang in Turkish
without accompaniment,
standing alone as if this were an interview
for residency.
And her wavered pitch contains every wired
vulnerability that a person who has been
wronged many times holds in perpetuity.
A monogamy of passion,
not to mimic the demands of fire but
rather a flickering resistance in all
dialects of the mother tongue.

I spoke briefly to her afterwards,
a few words of appreciation.
She understands.
Away from the stage, she lives in embers.
But compliments are an uncompleted circle.
A crescent to which she will have to return
pledging her voice to the all consuming choir.
Her eyes look not to the Tamar but out
beyond where the Bosporus flows a wide
water boundary from East to West.

The Pencil Maker

Where Leslie lives is only a hare's breath from
me but it might as well be Mars or far further,
a Galaxy for my mapping.

Every time I watch the ritual spreading of glue,
pasting papers, positioning the thin sticks
of graphite and clay to make up the lead pencils
I am drawn to this nimble fingered exercise
of long nails to knuckles and the way Leslie
licks each tip as if they were
French chocolat profiteroles.
And yes, I worry these pencils could be poison.
I say: Your tongue will go grey.
The reply: Your tongue will grow tired.

Afghan Rug

All those heroes
trying to weave the rug
of an elusive pattern of knots.
The dye boiled dry in Mazar-E Sharif
and the lie of the land buried thousands
beneath the steppe dust gravel after dogs
had gorged enough.

The child labour
working yarn reading a
palm and blunting the needle.
Exporting everything to Pakistan to
be relabelled: consumption by The West.
Talk runs a shallow stone river covered up
by an administration.

Sixty stick fingers
restoring the Quran for
the carpet. The beaten boy is
now learning his lesson in the latrine.
It takes sixty stick fingers to unravel this
error by the time terror dissipates the hand
of Allah upon his son.

And the daughter
of Allah, ah the learned
daughter, she who is greater
than a hundred suns, will tread softly
on the imported rug bought in Cambridge
for the price of a year's daily dumplings and
unleavened nan bread.

A proportionate
response arguably sized
to the room available at home.
Considering the intricacy of Islamic
design, geometry free of the human form,
there is much barter and haggling to be had
in the capital of Kabul.

Martha

She had not lived on her own for long.
Time was a cooking meal, culinary
in gratitude; a casserole of vegetables,
pulse and grains marinating in an oven.

Martha Gellhorn has avoided reading a
notebook for a decade or more; to
catch sight of her body-shape in bright
light is beyond the pale of recognition.

Full length mirrors might inadvertently
give up facsimiles of flesh. Sadly, if
she had only risked a glimpse it would
have been obvious that she possessed

undeniable arresting beauty within her
glaze-lines which made her all the
more beloved. Finely fashioned, as if a
ceramic figurine, enticingly blemished.

She knows war off by heart; describes
death of men and their battlefields
better than they could themselves. Yet
Martha had to beat a retreat eventually.

"It is too hard to sit on the outside and
watch what you can neither help
nor change." The outside, a place now
sick with the senselessness of butchery.

Her portable Imperial, typing massacre
from *The Besieged City*, writing to
fight fascism, key clattering act in *The
Face Of War*. Hell, bloody awful month.

Winter never got to know her well, not
in the ways she thought might be
possible when they had both visited in
the past. Winter became a blind beggar.

Her skirt neatly pressed into the crease
of its pleats, hangs discreetly just
below the knee. To repeat: "Winter will
never notice, winter has no eyes to see."

Firstly she's The War Correspondent yet
the whiff of wife takes the life out
of writing. Keeps her filling up whiskey,
cleaning male off the deck of the boat.

Killing time for the Spanish Civil War, as
the Catholic Church tolls the worst
wedding bells in their marriage of men.
"Never ever try to attach strings to sin."

And Hemingway's bloody bull ring ticks
off an afternoon cavorting tortuous
sacrifice. Always the animal; always the
brigade of recruits dancing left to right.

Now there were but few other voices to
tell her, "Martha, 'tis true you are
the only portrait in a crowded gallery of
miniatures." Gellhorn had already gone.

This time she saw no one in the room.
These were the years she gave to
herself an invisibility. A poltergeist life
preparing meals of vegetables and rice."

Mother Cancer crawls, fingering a wall
of blind alleys. What can't be seen
she tastes. Lack of appetite licking on
rice boiling burnt black in a saucepan.

Dedicated to the great writer and journalist, Martha Gellhorn.
(8th November 1908 - 15th February 1998)

The Alien Stranger

On the day they gave carnage to
America with the only god going
already gone suddenly it became
obvious this day too would pass

into a founding of imaginations.
Heaven was finally a fabrication,
an alibi for the end of the world.
There is no point in pretending.
Self protection balances on the
symbiotic empire of selfishness.
Preservation means beating the
border and retaining the power.

Keep it. Who requires a precious
casket of dust? These diamonds
in streams become the currency
of immigrants who had nothing.

Leaving is a terrible betrayal so
emphatic the Jinn gave up their
right to rent stars in Manhattan
becoming a dominion of actors

in this sad debris of belief. Test
every passing, constantly check
as if building a mansion on the
on the hill. The only god going

is fictional, it has no claim on a name. To lay the blame on such an arcadia is to reject symbiosis. Here the alien stranger is friend.

For Femme Affirm

Linguistically powerful is
no fashion accessory for personal counsel.
Rather, outspoken contemporary suffrage
offering a view but not the whole picture.
To believe anybody in that depth of detail
is irrespective of the affirmation.
I would if I could. If believing enough trust
was understood and freely given.
Rather than force singular into plural we
need new words free of genders.
They do not come this far in order to dress
to-be-seen. Colour code naked mannequins.
Far more than strength she has appearance.

Yes, they have appearance
and could easily flag themselves to address
the answer but not necessarily the question.
Every reply she has ever read is dangerous.
All eyes in their direction treated cautiously.
So she mixes genes with gender.
Stirs the witches' cauldron and strips away
illusion, rightly so in my opinion.
Of course they retain The Mystery Train.
No names are taken for granted.
Catches silk threads; unravel a hem's edge.
Then interpret sign of commitment in hard
softly spoken stories linguistically powerful.

In Those Halos Of Clay

Plant endangered species above
everybody's burial.
The legality of planting the past
deeply unarguable.
And the rising oceans waving at
submerged denial.
So grows a scattering of seed to
the blood vessels.
High tide carving away fossil in
those halos of clay.
So say the seas to fishing twine.
Tide takes time to
sink stuffed shirts in salty brim.
The gardening tip
of the day is to create drainage.
Water as required.

The Nib

The Nib moved to a new note book,
in those waking hours when
last night took to pen,
sitting upright like the judge about
to win a life sentence.

Hooded eyes, mouth dry tasting
of tin fillings, starved of a supper pup,
maple holding a thin stick sucking ink,
ear full of phone and static; pages
scratched with hieroglyphics,
decipherable as the diatribe of
a hundred straight unaltered words.

The Nib moved to a new note book,
waited awhile encouraging
the critical eye to look
for a sheet of famine to keep dry
the blot of the last full stop.

Ice/Acer

The miniature Acer had flamed
crimson, suntan crisping tips
of the leaves curling like curtsy
debutantes rooting a fertility
in an ericaceous establishment.
It is packed into a terracotta

pot with a lining of privet moss.
Back then a call and response
by nature to nature is grounded
to the fibrous cold membrane.
A Frozen fix, the blade of spade
breaks into its granular nerve

of sinew buried in the root-ball
block as if a forged sword has
exposed stone leaving a stump
dug out for replanting. Open
ground with gaping worm hole
receive this rooted tree whole.

The old wood worlds branching
April with a domesticated will
of their own. A house in human
form beneath the sickle moon
and tempt these crimson leaves
to leave as bright cut-out stars.

Discretion #

When we meet
and complete our exile
of each other it is a rare treat.
Reciprocity is not the rule.
As I sweep my floor every
morning greeting myself to
John Coltrane and lose
the stammer in my speech
I ask for nothing than music.

Twice a day empty a lifetime.
Let night be spent in sleep.
May the sun rise steep above
the moor and the rain moisten
my mouth to separate the stones
from the dip tic florescent sheep.
Let me laugh with my dear brother,
give love back to my daughters,
write them a weekly letter about
nothing and no one they need keep.

When they find a man upon my
seat let the muesli bowl be washed.
His life a neat ordered practice;
every yeah be yeah every no be no
and all enlightenment discreet.
As they wrap my body in a sheet
may it be the journey of a clean
ram setting out to seek the deep.

For Ferlinghetti

101
forwards then
backwards
into San Fran
the City Lights are
brighter & do not
cost The Earth.

3/1919 – 2/2021

Avon Dam

A loop of lettering sentenced
out of all recognition into a noose of numbers.
The spectacular statistics of mortality upon the body:
From heartbeat to heartache,
the pressure of pump and pulse, eyesight and earshot,
a blood clot count across a daily loss of skin tissue.
The ambient Avon hurling a mix of tinnitus over and
under a postcard's babbling brook.
Ganglia, holding ourselves in an embrace of aging.

The valley is invaded by purple
rhododendron; distress signals of an intoxication
wading either side of bog water paths, seepage from
the deep bed of soil's acidity.
Sheep shit-pellet droppings track the flat-rocks washed
continually by the transparent froth rushing river as
if racing against its fall to the sea. Water beats-up the
settlements of trough to trachea throat.
Ganglia, holding ourselves in an embrace of aging.

A thin screed of stones wrote
a trail's interpretation of routeing the Avon Dam.
I go there because I can and because trekking it takes
the landscape back for myself.
Makes amends out here with my legs walking the wind.
Sucking fresh air into breathing a tick, tick, tick of
where the heart has its own raging bull of matadors
piercing the sinews of calf and tendon.
Ganglia, holding ourselves in an embrace of aging.

Black Brake, Black Tor, Ryder's
Rings and the old stones of homes grown out of
the ground like birthmarks on the body. The Stretch
marks of a hotchpotch history
in every crevice and cave dent specter of burial mound.
And in that bent-leg-body is a starved pity for pain.
Here the cairn's executioner examines White Burrow
for a numbered noose of the hanging.
Ganglia, holding the number embracing our aging.

Apolitical

An apolitical person is not a political person.
An apoetical sentence is not a poetical sentence.
Reading poetry is apolitical.
So-it-was I got the message
that I make fun with words
but poetry is not for people to play with
in case it starts to catch the place on fire.

What would you have me do?
Sanitise each sentence for poetical content?
check that it has passed the rhyme this time?
Not mention Ginsberg for fear
I'll start howling at the moon?
Only read poems by Dickinson that have titles
therefore ensuring they are not blank verse?

An apolitical person is not a political person.
An apoetical sentence is not a poetical sentence.
Reading poetry is apolitical.
So-here's-a-thing that reads
well enough, take anger
out of the equation and it soon begins to
read as if it were apiece apoetry ablazing.

Volume

On the day he drank his last
mouthful of wine he did not know
it would be so.
For over thirty years a clear glass
each, every evening
at around the witching hour.
Two on a tray, sipped dry by two tongues
regularly attuned to the wet whistle
of Sauvignon Blanc, had now
suddenly gone astray.
A lack of volume in the bottle.

The first year of abstinence passed
by in a blur of starvation
and without incident.
Alcohol became tastefully redundant.
He no longer wanted to gargle it,
preferring the transparency of water.
There is no vice in volume
only in its capacity to speak louder
than the mind.
He is not sure whether his poetry
will continue to remain so sober
but for sure,
his drinking days are over.
At least for now.

He had not been getting pissed.
It wasn't as if his brain was stiff from
rioting in his own cell block number 9.
Or at least, not that I was aware of.
The grape had been pure pleasure
but like a lot of things there comes
a time when even the purity of pleasure
is only habit.

I simply didn't want to raise a glass.
I knew something else must come to pass
and so I took to breathing.

Darkmoor 8.00am

(i)

Monday, 8.00am, get-set-go into the
insistent boogaloo of James Brown's cold
sweat on the Ornette turnaround tuning of
broken shadows streaming for the inner lane
of the A38 travelling south sound to Plymouth.

Behind blows the spring blizzard
whirring wire, snapping the bent saplings
on the slope of the embankment.
Switch off the music and fossil fuel,
feel the weight of woodwinds inside
the diaphragm on Dart and watch flashing
finned skims of silver skin grayling.

I-spy-eyes watch the iridescent
damselflies hover paper-thin across the moss
stones and a film of jellied spawn.
This perforated place seen in a see-through
whistle of March-air smarts vision.
Within the hour the light whites
the porcelain sunken sink clear clean.
Please, let it be, brightly as green blown glass.
Please make it last, may reality be some kind
of finality, at least not seem a world away.

(ii)

An elderly mind continually
double-takes internally.
Pleads to the body's better self.
There is nowhere else to intercede,
this is where all old genders bleed.
But birds cease their acappella early.
Waking sleepers in the fog of gales
with what seems like a lost litany.
Deception flies in the face
of the sun striping 8.00am.
The hour-line cannot cast a shorter shadow.
James Brown was no morning man.
Here the residue of midnight is already dried,
daybreak broken into the earth.
One bird hears another and keeps schtum.
Even the uneven thought that has twisted a
blade in the dark now glints cold gold ready
to respond to the brown trout panicking in
a leat below the gurgle whirl of millstream.

This is where she met her Yoruba phantom
no longer in a foreign field.
Rolled up her sleeves and pulled the acrobatic
flapping fish out of its confinement.
Carefully carrying the creature slipping
and flipping, drowning in the open air placing
it back into the river-course to navigate again.
She left Lagos because Paris promised peace,
heals healers and protects leaders.
But the road to darkmoor was more
complicated than writing a PhD.

A Nigerian woman with the Rosetta Stone.
Her hand now constantly rests upon
his own stooped shoulder bone.
Home is a place that does not hurt.
In listening practice she hears the elements
in a Loose Tube saxophone singing early
for the primetime hour. Close enough
to count the new day number in multiple
keys of chorus and play one or two of these.

The Dart in diamonds
never flows this Tao again.
A stranger standing on the stepstone
in the middle of a running river looking for
what unaccustomed eyes can't recognise:
Whitman's world, a Dark Moor among white
lilies and wild garlic, swept aside the little
bridge of sighs where the Dart sends
pebbled gems west to the estuary's tide.

A territorial buzzard flies... by.
Glides with piercing eyes
across a scattering of sky
following a known contour.
Nothing strange to raptors.
                    The river the same sharp
line of prey whether dry or in full flood,
follows a curve, wide or narrow,
deep or shallow, given up to Gaia.
No Om
needs to be the centre of their own country.
Tap-roots can be ripped from beneath the feet
standing on a floor of concrete.

Here are ashes, blown whither the wind takes thee.
So flow the Dart and in the cold sweat of spring let
the new thing be a flowering through the frost;
and so another night lost taken on the wing.

(iii)

Being a buzzard is a measured migration
in the flight path to a bare nest of twigs.
The old bird with oiled feathers
shakes and shivers,
claws at the sinews until it can eat the liver
and the tiny heart still bursting with blood.
This is
a small circumference in chancel country.
A mile or two from the abbey; a stigmata
in the map stained with the piss of voles
and a wounded bat.
What holds the day below the night
enfolds life above the fray
ascending to a greater height.

(iv)

A muse can't always see that.
The whole day has been spent
bent over a keyboard tapping
tongues tucked into each page.

What would anybody discover
with such an agent of poetry?
A spy in the classic Mata Hari
sense of sensual description.

The Garden of Souls is a rural
tune Ornette rarely returned
to. Instead gathered notes as
men do when Eden is empty

of Eve and Adam. The digital
degree below zero requests
Stormy Weather – "There's a
sun up in the sky" exploding.

Here, fingers tap out regret
releasing the apple tree of
knowledge, forgetting what
wisdom it ever really knew.

Every bugalú bud morning
hands in its resignation as
a love letter. Slowly signs a
name; bird's pecking paper.

Darkmoor has risen across
a bright hale of noon. The
herd of deer have cropped
Bonehill of buried treasure.

They are nervous of canine
scent and smell the baying
dogs before those demons
bark and start to exercise.

This hard copy gathers the
occasion in lilacs of letters.
We wait for a wedding day,
postponed 'til forevermore.

"No, didn't bring diamonds.
I brought kiwi fruit instead.
To eat with the vinaigrette.
Let's talk as we taste them."

The bird has flown, chooses
to fly; cold as the godfather
of soul flows rock & roll off
boogaloo at Plymouth Hoe.

(v)

The reason for coming here was to hermit.
Not deny what had been, but to leave it.
True,
who can afford the price of permanence?
Maybe such an expense is an unholy noise
of money. Like jangling silver in front of
a beggared thief who has a hole
in each pocket as well as their heart.
In this case not even *The Garden of Souls*
is a place of pilgrimage. Those who would
do well would do better
to ignore such suggestions
and touch the Rosetta Stone.
Big Buddha is currently away on leave.
The buzzard left to blizzard the land
for a second or two scenting the quarry,
detecting the habitat of hermit.
A refugee will ask no more than to hold
shredded *Leaves of Grass* and wipe cold
sweat from where once they wept.

St Andrew's Remembrance

St Andrew's, Chew Magna; saltire cross
flag fluttering a not-so-ragged ribbon of
a fisherman a long way from the sea and
soon to be from me.

For thirty-four years I've watched over
this quiet granite weeded green garden
of remembrance, inhabiting the life ever
after Dhammapada.

Seasons: snow bound and frozen, late
spring-forward sprinkle the purple crocus
christening Chew Court Corner by a turned
and crooked stone,

summer shadow and light lined detail,
and come The Fall the great old weeping
ash shedding leaves as organic confetti in
October's raincloud.

Belief has carved the living and the dead.
Loaned to the soil and whittled out of the
yews. A ghost-free grave marking nothing
more than memory.

Yet we who have rooted ourselves to
this peaceful place of love and tranquillity
eventually will have to go toward the bells
tolling us to autumn.

Harringay

Yes, we were both born in Hackney.
In recognition break a cheese scone in two,
share it, taste tuppence worth of childhood
that was never going to last long enough.

The River Lea not as rich in rainbows
as the River Dart which parts company
with the castle coast at its darting mouth.
The Lea spills out into the Thames on a
curving current lapping the Isle of Dogs.

Harringay used to race greyhounds,
six hundred flat-capped scoundrels
bred to breed chasers on a wired windsock.
The sandpit track roar of odds lit light by
a bob or two on *Ballyregan Bob* and the
brindle dog comes in like he can't win-to-wait.
When they pulled the old place down and
built a supermarket it was bargain hunting
the hare for a piece of racing real estate.

We agree about improvisation
to such a degree it's an all round education
that's been Blurt and Pere Ubu mixed with
the same adult Dreamtime virile vinyl.
There comes a time when your ears grow so
accustom to wet and dry vocabulary it's like
translating the bookmaker tic-tac at Harringay.

Volans/Sleep/Poem

Volans' composition
is a description of the moment
in Nyanga music when instruments
cease to play, lay-down-the-line put
all melody away, leave only the
dancers' bells tied to their ankles
to tinkle in the night and thus the
White Man Sleeps.
Not in my experience.

Perhaps in Southern Africa, back
when black was neither here nor there
and white was the ruling class, sleeping
was possible or at least imagined to be so
by the 'boy' in the know
who was himself perpetually 'Watch'
working his eighty years of age
into the red earth of rough diamonds.
But he be Black with a capital B
and speaking such an observation would
get him a bullet for his bloody cheek.

Volans only made the music not the man.
And writing it down makes it no easier
to understand; harder
still is how anyone of whatever hue of colour
sleeps in the dark when the nightmare of not
staying awake is embedded in
each other's fear of one another.

Dedicated to the composer/musician Kevin Volans.

To Have But Not Hold

To have but not hold is eventually how
it has to be.
Sometimes to rhyme together becomes
the melody.
Sometimes to sing under the breath feels
as loud as opera in the overture, as if the
act of splitting song is the duet.

Spending so many hours composing a
musical score
when what is only understood are the
first four bars.
All subsequent attachment a thin shard of
sharps so lethal they need to be stored in
the heart to have but not hold.

Iwazaru

At no stage will war beat battles
but words can mitigate weapons.
Dumb silence in illicit innocence
is the first act in a theatre of war.
It becomes a terrible vow of void,
a scratched record of holy orders.

Skirmish after skirmish captured
in a lack of conversing. Violating
fighting talk, blurting out its own
wretched awfulness before being
spat back upon crap that killed it.
The wisest monkey Iwazaru talks

peace passing understanding, an
example of lucidity in disarming
this violence of silent incitement.
Iwazaru, who speaks no evil, will
continually chatter calmly calling
voices for people who have none.

The Golden Mean Of Mornings

(i)

I mistook what I heard to be
a human voice in counterpoint.
A Selmer soprano saxophone offers up
song through a reed cut precisely with
the clean edge of a new razor blade
as if fashioning a fly for fishing.

(ii)

Singing to an ear, blown on
a shaven smooth sliver of cane
pressed into lips as if a kiss articulates
the midpoint balance of noon, a twelve
to the power of the fledgling hours
in the golden mean of mornings.

(iii)

To sleep through the dawn
shortens half-a-life reclining in
enlightenment now already spoken for
rather than listening to the music from
a saxophone heralding a golden tip
of split animation on a cynosure.

Poet And The Hare

If ever a man had died
before he was ever dead
it was Dylan Thomas in America
reading what he had never said,
reciting verse he denied he read.
Mix mandrake in the Big Apple;
the great poet drank juice bled
from bottles bought in one bar
after another.
Wales, still an afterlife which
a dead poet cannot resurrect.

Beside the estuary at Laugharne
the long-eared hare holds up its
head sensing the air off the Atlantic.
The urgency of the animal
twitches in the direction of the wind
its frost fawn pelt prickles static
due west.
On such a day an uncertainty
of instinct finds a way through
the spinning weather vane.

The past cannot settle on today
because it has gone to earth
and doesn't recognise the speed
of the present tense.
No sense in going over old
ground except to shiver the
here-hare to leave the field

of bracken for a new habitat.
And so the Lepus go leaping
forward sniffing out the scent in
the fevered Bible black of spring.

Patience In A Sentence

To have patience is to
be patient with
the pen
write when
the mind can sign
its own reflection
not rush hand written
stereotypes into the
typeface ribbon
will only mulch
a rash across
the surface of a scrap
of paper to leave
an embossed
chipped letter
hanging in mid-tap
as the hand
falls slack what
must be left as
blank space intact.

Not-So-Far-Nirvana

Not-So-far-Nirvana is a short distance
to a narrow open door.
Short though an arduous journey.
A bent figure stands
begging alms for the entrance fee.
Hands cupped to collect.
Nothing given but hypocritical regret.
What once seemed like the other side of
Italy is as close to being believed as
intimately as breathing
is to the lip. What was once
bartered in Rome is now
stolen and measured out in bitcoin.

Not-so-far-Nirvana turns as familiar
as a book's blank page.
Everything else is promised land
sifting sand through
open hands pointing their palms
to a pilgrimage
of hermitage. As the door swings on
its hinges the bent alms beggar waves
us through, giving out free vouchers
so simple to redeem.
Yet as we now enter Nirvana
a receipt is read aloud as a
broken promise made in good faith.

Outtakes

In January 2021 during the bleak
peak of the pandemic I sit up late
listening to Bob Dylan outtakes:
a man who swears he's not to blame.
The room glows under linen light
playing through his contrite *hard rain*
as it strains to pour down
and explain the reasons why men bleed.
Oh mama, could this really be the end,
it's too late to say but I'll
tell you anyway. Its dark outside and
Santa-Fe is going to storm the Capitol.
Fully dressed and naked, there's
a man who swears he's not to blame.

And that acoustic guitar scratched
across a hollow body of Americana
continues strumming
shaking salt into an infected wound.
Bob Dylan's Dream,
Bob Dylan's Nightmare
to be a prophet with nothing to prove.
A hidden secret revealed in a room with
only one bulb burning before bedtime.

It's the last January I'll ever sit here.
Maybe next year I'll still be sat up late
somewhere else with another light
becoming dim as the thin man inside me
listens to a *Nobel-Laureate-Sings-The-Blues*
in whatever circumstances prevail.

There comes a point when the night
thickens calling pandemic time
on the arrival of the Golden Dawn.
I switch off the linen
plunging these outtakes
into the safety of darkness.

Waiting With Beethoven

Waiting with Beethoven
to string things together
into a row of beans in early Spring.
Their shells tap on his table.
Percussion, always his strong
point even with the bow of the viola.

For things to germinate
here the alchemy of water
and heat tuned to each deft stroke
completes a growth seedling.
Rise to the cosmos or lie down
in the soil and grow into the graves.

Not here, not now, but
at noon someone tries to
buy thirty five years of dividing the
tranquility, but we will sell to
him as if giving ourselves away.
Grow tough tympani tissue in our ear.

Why trouble a composer
to listen? After such silent
music, what can be heard that has
not already been rehearsed a
hundred different times before?
Best leave Beethoven to grow Allegro.

Eye of Faith

In all good faith
a pen of calligraphy
shapes the art of letters
angled and argued over with
the blunt instrument of rationality.

Straight strokes of luck, divinity draws
icons into every corner of the page.
They, whoever they are, cannot say
who wrote what when before Christ.
As if Allah, Shiva, Brahma, Vishnu,
Siddhartha Gautama and all the other
prophets of this world's word were an
ancient arc too long in the curve of time
they fold into one another as an invented
alphabet. Such men committed nothing
to paper.
In an eye of faith each one of us purports
a vision. In lettering them, produce
pictures more groundbreaking than
the magic of their miracles.

And so I ask all of you who once claimed
insight into those eyes of revelation,
see me in the watermark indentation
buried deep beneath handmade paper.
For in there resides a sight of faith,
a fleck of ink that sparkles a dark mark
brighter than gold. So, an old tarnished
world carries its daily text trails of emoji,

utterly disposable. Easy eyes easy lies, yet
there is a vision in the slipstream. Word
of mouth
spoken with intention to sustain a secular
faith and if I can retain anything give
me the insight to an invented alphabet
recognisable to my own name.

The title is borrowed from Professor Mary Beard

Po/Hymn

"Abide with me fast falls the eventide.
The darkness deepens Lord, with me abide.
When other helpers fail and comforts flee
Help of the helpless, oh, abide with me."
Henry Francis Lyte/William Henry Monk

Hear the scratching at the back door
and the flapping fur of feathers
against skin but never let Lucifer in.
Such a beast is only a wings-width away
from a crawling bird dragging its damaged
death knell behind, rattling a clanging bell.

To live with Lucifer is to have a thorn
beneath our fleshy fingertips.
Press on it and every small
insignificant prick asserts pain
with minimum of effort.
A tic buried into shit.
Growling beneath the surface,
cutting the corners, inflicting
a nonstop plop, plop, plop of bile
as if bile be blood and blood be
green with envy.

The portrait is sketched with strokes
in a cross-hatched pencilling.
An angel's face via memory
identifies a devil quicker than
inventing another name

to add to the religious litany.
Picture the pinched eyes and
cruel mouth shut tight, tight shut
in an effort to disguise what is
green with envy.

Light repels the demon angels.
Spring greenery must abide.
Fast falls these old devils when
they dive into the eventide.

On A South Bound Train

When that one old woman dies
a history of a hundred lives dies with her.
Honey, this isn't saving a sliver of her skin.
Nope, this is about owning our own and I don't
care whether you-be black, brown or white
what's in her history is gonna make your mind
turn in its archive like the wheels
on a south bound train.

History ain't a broken rail if we
know the tracks taken by all the precious
people who built meaning into liberties. If
history is just a mystery we too become ghosts
to our purpose, so I'm asking everyone to
collect yesterdays as they edge forward in the
queue that waits to board for a ride
on a south bound train.

She is the key that unlocks the
carriage door for us to enter. She held in
her head torn, scuffed sepia prints of map
and journey. This is our train to travel, this is
the past that points to the horizon; ignore
one old woman and lose the whole edifice of
everything that makes for climbing
on a south bound train.

For Maya Angelou

Spores

So easy to pick out at any corner store
bouquets of cut tulips already no more
than a week away from fading colours.

The bank below the football pitch has
grown a stitched evergreen patchwork
that could cover up the whole country.

Soft shield ferns caught and grounded
brown by sunlight spores in the border
to multiple beneath the long leaf flax.

Planting does not stay still, the pursuit
of shade, constant reproduction when
left to follow the pageant of hedgerow.

These Jacaranda Trees

A new garden instead of an
undergrowth of briar weeds
and twisted roots there is a
field full of blue cornflower.
She bends over, picks them.

A vivid colour of coppice is
the borderline. I will grow a
rebirth without you cutting
down these Jacaranda trees.
They are our skirted sisters.

I now understand it was not
of my doing but something
you needed to complete for
yourself; the blue blooming
far too brightly blue for you.

Like the Jacaranda came out
from the jungle, we all once
grew our way through green
landscape to reach daylight
and came coloured by blue.

Wishing On Washington

"*I wish I had a river to skate away on.*"
So sang Joni back before the glacier
melted. Long time ago, when fears
of an avalanche only stretched
as far as Vietnam.
This Christmas the river
has not frozen over.
There will be no skate-dancers
screeching retreat on blade scratch lines.
Today the ice rink river is a running tap
of soap suds and cinema chains.

Bilingual blue to bleue covered in mill waste
and the buttoned-up girl 'skating away' is
replaced with walking hand to mouth on
a terrain of road blocks to Washington.

Not quite as unrequited as lovers from
a past unimaginable today. Time was
when a Madonna was unable to lay in
the shallows without drowning
her baby before it
was even borne away. In
the frozen waters of
the Columbia River where the
walkers practice to play their long lines
they are collecting samples to test the
waters for pollutants and algae.
The three wise men are come to forever
interpret the ice before it ends up as the
generous interpreter of them.

In Ratio

When night turns to curve
in ratio it reflects inside
a low glow of solar
no need of mass.
The lone star to the long star,
how short a time for the light
in the shade of other people.

For the way of stars is a striped
white-world circling the somewhere
self cannot make for reservation.
Continually they clean the litter from
the river at the end of the road.
In doing so it becomes a quiet revelation:
Where there is no way
there will be a way.
When that final journey comes
it is a privilege to remain in ratio.

Our faces scanned with a scientific dignity.
Nobody able to explain exactly who they
are, a trail defined yet remaining empty.
By any stretch of an imagination starry,
starry burnt too bright to last eternity
open to the library of deity theology
that consumes and imbibes the sky
in light years of brief existence.
Does it matter, this dark matter?
Sometimes a way comes
out of the air to spot us.

Rita Dove

By burning books they have burnt
the authors too.
How long before they come to set
afire the readers?
Believers who thought this worth
their time's eye;
to the letter that is what they do.

Not simply singe each sentence
but crush ash within every page
of their argument and hostility.
Burn all eye-balls, trace a paper
trail through this knowledge of
what blinds them; yet we retain
a faculty of vision. Despite their
pyromania we publish, we print,
we write it down with bitter ink
and I open a book by Rita Dove
alive to its eternal possibilities.

Willy Staey

No protection for Willy Staey.
Coming and Gonne is not the same
as the next man born on the bend of the road.
No country for old men in the mire,
is that not right Willy?
Will-he-stay? No nor even his bones leave
a firm grave of certainty
because that is the way of it.
There is no protection from the indignity
of death and of all men this was one who
had come to know that the final act of bravery
is to stay alive as long as either hand will write
it down to fight a corner of the crumpled page.

For Willy Staey even scribing
his own elegy is a necessity. Leave
that to chancing his arm and grave bones are
robbed of a peaceful place in a pit
dug in heaven's earth.
"He is a fool, a fob of a god of graphics."
And so it is, the prize 'tis
proffered in another country
but argued over at home like meal tickets.
Better buy news than food to fill the belly.
A critique invents the hook to hang a poem on.
A barb at an easy idiot; he wrote for the occult
and the witchcraft magic of charlatans. There is

no protection for Willy Staey.
Because it takes practice to miracle
the years. Imbibe them with a comprehension
of what it is to love, man or woman,
ragged or rich, kept in
the calling with this intemperate speech.

Walk away from him but
he will never walk away from
you. Willy drew his vast map of membrane,
sun and moon born in an eternal marriage.
Consummated by being, passing each other in
a pattern of interdependence of independence
which has no protection, is that not right Willy?

Athletes

Athletes running pass me breathing dusk
fast and free of anyone, leaning into their
legs, feet drumming a choir of percussion
on the earth as if the ground were hollow.
I look away, no trust in the air between us.

I am bundled and buttoned up against a
spittle of the sky, only my eyes open, slit
into scars fixed in the little cusp of light.
Lids pressed into the racing evening and
the glass misted up breathing in a mask.

The wave of my momentum is with them.
Speed the runner on and let none get as
near as the fear of sharing another slice
and second of space. Let the intermittent
shower wash away such intimate contact.

Red Planet

They had been playing *Red Planet*,
taking the sonic trip up and outta
space to where few people want to go on
a Saturday night when the world collapses
around the end of the evening.
Midnight soaked in neon gets no one near
the surface of Mars
never mind a miracle of music.
For sure Coltrane had always treated
the twelve tone like a mode; fact, he sometimes
named it as that but Pee Wee's Bb licorice clarinet
would have none of it; already leapt the line
like jumping gravity when a rainy night
suddenly warms up.
Heaven knows who hears
the God of War as the God of Good and Evil
but by 1962 when Pee Wee Russell touched
down with the tune no ears were arguing
with what they could hear
coming out of the ancient *New Groove*.

There are only so many bars in the
City of Soho as Ronnie pertinently
pointed out to no particular person other
than those of us who already knew how to
steal a scene. See a mind's eye
that is what the Great Observatory has
hit upon, more red,
less grey, blue to green and a
colony of music as ancestral as Africa.

So you blow dry wood through reeds like over
wide plains and across this Serengeti of chorus
and who is to translate what-when-how-but
Pee Wee understood about *Red Planet*.
What we still believe
when catching a phantom
haunting the horns of Shabaka Hutchings
knowing it to be a real new thing orbiting
what we came here to do. Forget no one
least of all Pee Wee Russell
who saw the comet coming before us.

Largo Ren

You may rob the Three Armies of their commander,
but you cannot deprive the humblest peasant of his opinion.

Before you embark on a journey of revenge, dig two graves.
The Analects of Confucius

They seek no revenge.
Why would they dig their own hole
when there is a chance to build a new house?
We know knowledge eats the soul if it is not
told truthfully and freely.
They seek no revenge
because robbing three armies of
their commander was not a prime occupation.
Now there can only be opinion left and deprivation
of opinion will never conquer three armies.
Good as they are, these people will stop at nothing
to surrender a soft beater to the slow, slow
movement towards a stroke of luck on taut tympani.
It is read, anyone who leaves without explanation
has already told themselves how to swing in rhythm.

A Man Who Closes His Eyes

A man who closes his eyes lies down
in the shade of dusk.
"It is a kind offer but I wouldn't want to
share a bed for just one dark sleepless night
as much as I might like to see the stars ignite.
To touch and be touched in the soft satin spot
for a brief moment would hunger me for what
has gone, there is no point in that fading light."
A man who closes his eyes can rest them.

Catherine Wheel

We talk because we share stories
and go to sift through the content
to read the next installment before
being confident who holds the blue
fuse twist of narrative.
Always unlit literature comparative
to those fireworks spinning sparks.
We cannot console our scars without
reading the chapter on Joan of Arc.
It might be easier holding each others
hand to comfort the brand mark of arson.

But that is not going to be how it
is, we know we remain inflammable.
My eye might be a little crooked but
not so unaligned that I cannot curve
away from her anatomy.
Curl paper into this betting slip that
buys enough time to turn a roulette.
Come, all fingers and thumbs into the
sparking story of blazing fireworks.
Not too late in the day to spin circles
for a Catherine Wheel's dazzling display.

The Cuckoo Not The Crow

She remained a woman open to the elements.
Headscarf wrapped over her house of hair,
tied-in under the jaw, parched throat gagged
against weather men she would never see.
That much was obvious, they came to collect
her confession regularly at intervals of vision.
She, too expensive for their stupidity.

Her wing feather fan closed.
Trapping talk in error, tapping her shuffling
walk away from these debt collectors.
Able to detect doubt impersonating a shout
grasped out of ornithology; two dots for idiots.

She heard the hesitancy freezing in the breeze;
blowing a terrible tease of uncertainty rupturing
into her blur of birds.
Such is the inked in code of birthmarks.
A / fee / male; constantly reproaching herself
with an identifiable repetition of regret.
Striking her speckled breast in a nest of rhythms
in a hurry to receive an answer by return.
Eventually she spoke, in a voice unheard before:

"I am so sorry my love,
I never meant you not to know.
This was a secret that cages
the cuckoo not the crow.
And though I peck at the coded row
of letters in your name they never spell true.
Who are you to call me mother?"

The Golden Mile

Basmati rice,
walked the Golden Mile,
Basmati rice,
walked the Golden Mile
left the candyfloss behind
and ate the curried dhal.

A short but detailed journey, it cannot be hurried, every step pressed under foot with precision. It is a route that will only be walked once in any life. Commit to it and there is never room for a return.

Every weekend we went to the arcades with cheap trash as prize money playing Wayne Fontana and The Mindbenders instead of The Stones. Helter Skelter carried us by air into the Crooked House.

Agra by the River Yamuna, white and lit like cake. Shah Jahan built it for his wife's body but kept a place for himself and walked the Golden Mile. They eat Basmati rice in Agra like Victoria sponge.

Pauper

Pauper is no longer a word in common usage.
Bankrupt vocabulary, not a word to be played
with or swallowed whole. Unlikely to occur
in the parlance of polite conversation
even less in shit street where beggar and
thief will mug the rough sleeper's dog money.

From poor to pauper is not the meagre mile
between alliteration and a damp sheet.
Jenny Pauper may be poor but she can still
sew up the hole in her breast pocket.
Except there's a dearth of needles and cotton.
But she breathes her own air as long as she's
not trespassing. Knows how to sell her sister
because she did so a good decade ago and
it isn't funny anymore.

Pauper is not a word that everyone is going to
thank you for. It is so embarrassing to have it
raised at a time when we are all struggling
with denial or denying we have a lack
of the wherewithal to even cover ourselves
up and make a decent stab of just pretending.

Pauper came cut into a Victorian gravestone.
Each letter paid for with a stolen bible
taken from the chapel. The cheap kipper has
no holy bible, no Quran, no literature
of faith or allegiance. There is nothing to steal

and nothing to take away. Here have a night's shelter and shower, split the profit on a punt they are going to deep clean the carpet and turn your salary green.

Convalescent

This morning she has not yet soaped
herself of the cotton sheets, there is no hurry to do so.
She can nurse that second weak Darjeeling and gaze
head bowed, eying the bowl of the cup to observe
a spread of leaves mapping her means of meditation.
Even at this early hour sat in a chair her spine stretches.

The light behind her eyes rises slowly
as day breaks into convalescing. From what ailment,
it is much too hard to explain; possibly the rash of
shadows is the fever we all fear. At the time she
could not speak of quarantine or quantify protection.
She never meant any harm, only that they both be free.

All diagnosis unacknowledged platitude,
the buried pain endured like the portrait in its frame.
She sips, sits, recalling the half smile, strange there
is no enquiry about the grief. They always want
detail of her heart but never ask anything that brings
relief; the painted canvas yellows the colour of her skin.

The Abbey

The Abbey grew out of fields, taken to fresh air
where stone and mortar could breath.
Bees make honey, there's a gigantic buzz about
this place which wills prayer to be as sweet as honey.
Anybody could be buried here as long as such details
are unknown, only revealed at the night of resurrection.
By which time too late for a substitution.
And this is the Abbey. The woman wearing a headscarf,
holding her patios bible close to her heart, praying out
loud with softly spoken urgency is told:
"Please be silent sister."

The Abbey bells ring for the whole world, toll for
the money, peal for complaints, sing for a
recommended donation of 10% of waged income.
The 'wages of sin' will be accepted provided they are
consecrated according to the traditions of the church.
Prayer is strictly the private providence of each sinner's
soul and the Lord of Love who judges the
living and the lived. The woman walks through the nave
with her sweetheart of beeswax intact to offer up gentle
whispered supplicants to a Babylon priest:
"Please be silent Honey."

The Swan In The Evening

Fondly they had watched together
as the swan in the evening
moved over the lake.
In the air the great bird's wings throbbed
back and forth, back and forth
with all the energy of departure.
Gaining in dynamic,
the long outstretched neck
pointing toward them from across the water
they could hear nothing else.

At the moment of passing
an incantation in the air:
It will not be long love. It will not be long love.
It will not be long love. It will not be long love.
Then that fragment was over as if the flight
of one Mute Swan had flapped
a thunderous way into folklore over night.
And the whole shimmering lake lapped
as if to imitate the great bird's bell-beat wings.
And he turned, instantly realising
she had stepped away.

This poem is a reimagining alluding to the lyric
by Herbert Hughes
of the melody of She Moved through The Fair.

Meals

1970

Lunch came with all the trimmings;
mountains of roast potatoes high
as the Himalayas with onion gravy
like a heated glacier and breast of
lamb minted lean; slow tenderised
cooking piled on a plate to celebrate.

2010

Picnics were a particular speciality.
Falafels nestle next to handpicked
truffles, strips of raw vegetables and
apple with a small pot of saffron-dip
in which to finger feed with flatbread;
cubes of fresh lemon to suckle taste.

2020

One small bowl of leftover rice, an
old orange, peeled by a blunt knife
and a cup of hot water given time to
cool. This would be enough for now
and later could be later still; already
it ceased to really matter any longer.

Four Storylines

In Slovenia, a far distance from his
native Cornwall cradle, Jack is outside hid in
the wind wrapped up like a peasant farmer poet
with words to spare and scatter.
Today he is spreading wet sodden leaf mold
onto his fields, mulching the grounding
of existence from a wheel barrow that rattles
and rolls tracks across the sloping contours
of tree-line, skyline and hill.
This is his whereabouts, no doubt his storyline,
sink his root crop in Slovenian soil
while practicing the language.

In Normandy the coast is closed to all
except the seabirds rising and falling on the
old rope oyster beds calling for fishing, missing
the strolling presence of Parisians
who once visited them. Madam Aubert sits at
the window watching the waves beat back
and forth until the beach is covered by the tide.
She has been continually drinking cold café
from the same yellow cup.
This is her whereabouts, no doubt her storyline,
a bitter taste of coffee bean stirred
into broken soaked biscuit.

In Arizona a cattle ranger tells Myrie
that he does not judge immigrants by where
they come from; only by intention can you know
someone's faith for good or ill.

Today the old cowboy is separating his calves
from the cows, "Yep that's okay for these
animals but you don't do that to children and
mothers. Deliberately orphaning a child cuts
up families like a head-of-steers."
This is his whereabouts, no doubt his storyline,
a man whose complexion has been
weathered by the right thing.

In London Nancy is only visiting her
bubble, heaven only knows who dreams up the
terminology in this nightmare of global pandemic
crisis, it certainly wasn't Nancy.
Two weeks juggling grandchildren isn't blowing
bath bubbles, isn't drawing portraits onto
handmade paper, isn't reading Helen Dunmore.
Two weeks of kicking fallen leaves in the park
and feeding ducks brown bread.
This is her whereabouts, no doubt her storyline
but not a narrative she has any need
to copyright for uncertainty.

Tabularasa

In the last six months he began to get the hang of how critically significant his role had been. Residing here alone; having had his life become legal property he paid cash to get it back again. The walls would continue to stand upright if he kept painting them which he continued to do at slap dash speed on Friday afternoons.

However much domesticity was applied it could never quite be enough. More cleaning, more repairs, additional making-do with secrets built into the fabric of the place as if a fitted kitchen was an essential performance space for the whole family. By his own admission the portrait of the man was flawed; lost and found.

This period became his Tabularasa, to attempt his own possession of potency and planning charting on a route to new residency. There is no escaping, he alone had to clean the slate if there were to be any chance of maintaining himself. Cracks in the walls collapse head and home. Not even he waits indefinitely.

To bury Tabula beneath a brain covers up the past as if merely old regret to be wrapped and put away in memory. All his friends, and he has many, have mourned with him of the passing. Yet in the cold light of day there is no other emptiness other than Tabularasa. A hole in thin air is constantly filled.

Chapatis

In October 2020 I quickly cooked chapatis
listening to Coltrane's *Acknowledgement*
out in Antibes in 1965.

The tenor refrain became like the flipside
of my hand. The few minutes on the hot
griddle fixes the flour,

oil, salt and water transforming flatbread
into a meal with scrambled egg, all over
in the time given up to

a saxophone extending the sonic season
of a *Love Supreme*. Hungry, yes but I am
also about to play for time.

The clocks took an hour out in the middle
of the night and so this morning I reason
those intervening years to

be the mathematical sum of counting me,
Chapatis, Coltrane and whatever remains
the perfect accompaniment.

Albino Tableau

The pure Albino bird
inherited whiter white.
Now flies the rest of life
free of other colours.

No rest can be the present.
There is no given gift to bring.
Pink eyes blink blue into mist
see whiter still and

curate a caged aviary
for this Albino Tableau.
On the line of Lagos bay
is a vision of Ulysses.

Medals/Cakes

They looked like a row of medals
on a flat chest veteran's breast;
six decorated cup cakes
in red, white and blue icing
dusted with chocolate flake
each one with a whole glacé cherry
sat right on the top.

Rita had brought me this tray of cakes
on no particular day of the year
saying, "Girls on pensions must bake
for each other and taste a little luxury."
For the next six evenings
I savoured one cake to the last crumb
gently humoured by sips
of fragrant elderflower.

Normally I would avoid sugar
in the same way as I pass on men.
Six cakes cannot defend their actions
but we are all veterans of old wars,
so we occasionally, award medals.

Monochrome Phone Photograph

On the right of the bend
where the hills open out
the trees hang monochrome
against the water in the sun.
The narrow road bends
behind them as if there
is some purpose in
travelling beyond and below
the dark spindly arms of leaf wrist
bark flagging down the road.

There is no one standing
shaded by monochrome
beneath the Beech. A bend in
the road curves, a bent wire
fence keeps nothing out
and nothing in, a picture
carries no sound and
sound no picture but is cast in
the light elemental spread on sky as
a cracked cloud kissed by cold.

Anglican Advent

How long is the length of love?
Eternal.
No, no, love comes and goes.
As in all things love exists
for as long as
it clings to the heart of the messiah
and is freely given up to liar to liar.
But in our ecology we squander
what matters most in the world.
When night passes the rotation of
Planet Earth's orbit to be replaced
by day it is a stretch over seasons
and reduced in the dust of more
than we ever know.

So what then is the eternal life?
A myth.
No, no, it exists in the space
of universal infinity but is
that what the
questioner asks of love of another?
Each Magus consults astronomy.
Love has a mask, form, emotion
and power. Advent comes again
like a blazing flame. And we warm
to holy ground of lockdown staked
in the wake of fire. Given residency,
a silent virus demands us to count
the cost of loving.

If I Am Ravenous

Dogs will eat a dog if they become hungry enough. If I am ravenous tearing and biting the split nails from my own withered hand becomes but the beginning to persistently consuming the whole elbow.

Once warring males are on heat they are a bone away to feasting on humanity. Sanity is decimated with debris of bloody divinity scattered across the floor of the cave as if the goodbye is already gone.

There is no 'if' about any of this behaviour or its result. Of course the dog is ravenous and obviously will return to lay waste to the pack of starving men. There is no goodbye proffered in the parting shot.

You can pray to Peter, you can pray to Paul but neither will eat the dog that kills us all. The heart is the last part to be torn from a canine body by its own breed but it bursts goodbye long before we feed.

Hospital Rose Garden

Small rose garden, a wall shielding a need
not to be noticed under the trees. All eyes
towards a constant stream of ambulances
reversing the flow of masked disease and

sickness clouded in headlines. I sit beside
the hand-me-down rucksack which used
to belong to someone called Theo. How
it came into my possession is lost within

the perennial border. Here on a dry teak
bench dedicated to a Dr J. E. Cates, born
1914, deceased 1994, this old blue bag
is to all intents and purposes mine. The
September cold peaks early, no roses in

bloom. They have been carefully pruned
and like a skilled biopsy with knowledge
of a need to prepare for hibernation, we
too must consider what requires cutting.

The Depth Of Winter

This solstice does not offer peacemakers.
Scrubland burns, a charred hand turns up
the heat on fire and brimstone.
Scorching an elemental meltdown
of frozen spillage through this viral
winter's groundings is what we do;
as diver, diver dives hoping.

Somehow I suspected it would come this
winter, at least I feared so.
My father had fallen the equivalent year
and though I do not believe the ice
breaks twice in the same place
experience tells me
where there is still water
expectation is not a poor fool's folly.

The world looms large enough
for a myriad of translucent tales
and we are susceptible to such stories
when the nights draw in.
This year I know I grow small into the
hollow foundations of a shared home-turf
dug below any whim of wind stroking the
stability on the far bank of the mighty lake.

When diving as deep as we have dived
I hope the ripples do not reach out to
touch the living you have on the other side.

The world looms large enough for a diver's
body to ache and arc with dire warnings.
We break surface shivering a layer of skin
against the grain of the jetty.

What gets me gets you,
is that your worry?
What comes for me will not be satisfied?
Winter will stake out your frozen frailty
and find a thin melt-water around you?
I understand;
at this time of the year beware the diver
who breaks the ice without meaning to go
as far down as the matted
thick green weed at the depth of winter.

Dancing On Dartmoor

"No one does the polka up here.
We needs to picks our way across
this loose scree or you
be slipping and missing your feet
and then the whole house comes
down, don't it.
I mean in the doings of a fall
anyone can lose all
they've ever wanted by fidgeting
on slopes of rocky rabbit-run.
I suggest not so much as looking
where you be going but, seeing
the sights before you trip
the light fantastic."

And instantly there's a knowing glow
of what is being talked about as each
letter switches on a sense of meaning.
The dancing high moor mountaineers
stand still, stopped in their tracks,
surveying the arrival
of the morning sun.

That Morning At Sandycove

That morning he had shaved his face
to the point it looked into the Atlantic
Ocean and tasted exile on the surf.

That morning he had begun the tale
and knew as clear as sunrise it would
end by evening's continuous elegy.

That morning she was already to go
the full distance and did so with ease
lifting the latch before he realised.

That morning had been rehearsed in
her head, planned like a dead weight
to be carried and buried in the Liffey.

That morning Odysseus was named
anew and given the run of the capital;
written into Dublin like a paid debt.

Stephen's Portrait Of James Joyce

Winnigan's fake portrait is a genuine
picture of all the paintings of the Liffey
running under the Ha'penny Bridge and
out through Dublin's fair city to the
drowning salty Irish Sea.
Anna Livia Plurabelle, haloed be her
eve upon his choppy whirlpool waters.
We have come here, not to swoon
on a woman but to swear on the
word of Joyce who gave birth to her.
Quote a verse of the moon upon
a moonless night with the snow falling
all over Ireland like a dense poem of prose.

And we know Winnigan must be Finnigan
wide awake at his own funeral party.
So we celebrate his living with a shilling's
worth of unrhymed monologue.
Drinking all the porter in the leftover
glasses he spies with his un-patched eye
a day in the life of a people as married
to fact as they are fiction and fable.

Annah the Allmaziful, a reen of river cut
below the hill where the abandoned
Hero picked up his pen to write himself
and everybody else into what has
become the lyricism of literature
as lucid as St Patrick's Day.

Truth is genuine enough when left to
stand for awhile without the pale frothy
topping spilling over the glass.
And the Liffey flows inside Dubliners
like a plate of eels for supper.
But trying to spy water snakes
in the middle of Ha'Penny is much too
hard a task for anyone and a genius
like Buck Mulligan vomits up limericks
at the first sight of supper.
The man hops on his heels
as if his stomach were on the fiddle.
What use is food without a
lather on the glass?

No answer Nora, no answer,
the portrait is only a dancer
but words in your ear
are nothing to fear,
Joyce's jig is a chance for a chancer.

I-Pretend-I

It is like Christmas in a cave of cut
chestnut and withered white ash.
I-pretend-I
can survive, live a backwoods life
when all the time I'm itching to
sweep up the earth and plant an
ochre carpet stitched of fallen leaves.

Each ant is my friend and the flies
mean no harm. In their habitat
I-pretend-I
will be able to make simplicity a
stone sculpture, instead a rock
between a hard place and wood
soft with dew is the bed I sleep upon.

The rough sleeper with the word in
one ear hears the blue tit tuning.
I-pretend-I
recognise the morning evidence
of that shrill hymnal harmony.
A birdlife language translated to
nothing I know except the thrill of it.

Maestro

Keith, how well did you know our man Danny?
I mean, as you have come to know him now.
It seems to me he was always part of you in
a manner of speaking.

As your piano is now his instrument of choice
because you play the high note with the low
and know Patrick O'Gonogon like an author
recites his own words.

May you say an Ave Maria for me Keith, when
the time comes I will applaud you as always.
You my dear friend, when all the flowers are
dying, live among us.

And so it seems to me that at Piacenza in the
January of 2012 when you dare to quote the
Londonderry Air as if its birthmark was just
another act of bravery

your intention was to grace a piece of history
on the line for all to hear; that is *Danny Boy*
your companion in sunshine and in shadow,
spontaneous in music.

For the great pianist Keith Tippett, my friend and buddy.
(25th August 1947 - 14th June 2020)

A Small Thimble

A small thimble for a fat finger,
hallmarked silver for the best protection.
In truth it was only jammed on to stop
the slipping needle continually pricking
his bouzouki playing hand.

As long as it gets done,
it matters not how;
poor commentary, not worth a penny.
Surely we would want to make the night
as beautiful as the stars.
Six years ago he would have sipped
a lick off the rim of flavour for himself.
He had seen her sipping a thimble
of white wine casually as if it were water.

"Why not a small thimble to toast the
bride and swallow the sweetheart?"
The lilt of Dublin in the questioning
adds to the hint of his temptation.

Whatever he now brings to the
marble table is unfermented,
not a case of needless sophistication
clearly all such considerations are cured.
This is about the simplicity of love.
A small thimble for a fat finger
is a relatively inexpensive precious
thing and allows his old withered hands
to touch her neck and shoulders
with a measure of sensitivity.

"A small thimble, is that all it is?"

This Long Distance Call

If I understood
and could be consistent over time.
Not let myself go like a stone dropped
from a height I will never reach
then the width of this ledge
would not scare me to hell.
It's brevity that denies a long distance call.
As a soliloquy of poetry, I'm reading it out
loud on the phone to make more miles fall
like the smallest avalanche.

Requiem Sharks

Below our boat's bow deck
requiem read the sea.
We study stars above
the Gulf of Mexico to the Florida Keys.

In the moon-tide's hunger for oceans
French requin, ruin and in rune
shark the shallow sound.
Wind over waves across the bay
rim-a-reach of concentric circles
round the ink blue deep.
Dorsal fins silently signing the surface
stir below the waterline wreckage for
sailors perished by tempest in temptations
to the vast Pacific Ocean.

Sieve plasticity through this body
of water crewed by fishermen, plankton,
elasmobranchii, porpoise, whale and
slow boat fishing rod.
Eyes upon each other, interpreting the
watchful signs in the channel's reflection.

Requiem Sharks turn on such timings.
Back and forth on their perpetual search
for the food chain's indelible link
between their sunken underworld
and the bleep-bleep-bleep of satellites.

Blue Rosette

He hadn't realised it was to be
such a cattle market of slobs.
What men, penned up as if anyone unworthy
of the terminology, are going-to-want-to
buy and flog a bull for its own sake?
Caught, measured by size and shape,
check the teeth for aging, their minds for decay.
And as they lean over the rails to pick up the
auction money the pretenders are left to stand
awhile so someone can squeeze what disease is
beneath their doubled entrails.

The karat of each gold earring
and the intensity of blue ink in
the tattooed eagle on his arm compared to
the faded sparrow on his arse masks his
inadequacies spread over the body
like a glue of bones. Judge this one
against the copy-cat, is there another version?
Has he got a younger brother in the back of
the trailer in the yard? Maybe we could shave a
bit off the price if he were described as being of
'pensionable age' with income.

He's not the first lover to turn up
with a blue rosette in hand and be
put out to grass. As quick as a man comes to
the door he gets a round of applause from
tipsy rabble but bulls like him are not soft
seduction speculation. There is a scent of

spent fireworks about him; a tame dragon maybe, but not a stud with a blunt nose for trouble and strife, you understand? No one fetches what they are worth and what they eventually sell for comes contrary to appearance.

Charterhouse

Mother, rainfall has collected in these puddles
of the sun marrying mirrors on coal slag chips
across Charterhouse. I believe we brought you
here when you were a little child and a shower
of rain could still bring warmth to your skin.

You, forever skipping in the sunshine's lantern.
Foraging for friendships with insects, speaking
to them and translating their replies because
we were too big to hear their child-size voices.
Already you knew the difference between too

big and too small. Nuggets of clinker become
nuggets of gold and you weaved a story about
how this is a special one. You could give it to
your mother as a present because she would
want to see it glitter black in the colour of her

hand and grip it's sharp edges in her gentle
palms. At least that's what I took you to mean.
You were chattering in streams it was difficult
to tell but this was the gist of it. So oblivious
to the rain you said the sky was spilling water.

Nun

No one has touched me
and I have touched no one.
Instead tiled surfaces are softly stroked like
the skins of domestic animals.
I lean on the lives of other people.
I lean on lay people's confessions
only to find them bend under the pressure
of the absence of caress and reshape their
hands into the folds of my dress habit
spun from calico thread.

Of course they do; my experience
is not unique to me, we are touched by the
Dutch courage of our calling, we might not
all fall in exactly the same direction
nonetheless we must all fall.

No one has touched me
and I have touched no one
and in my elopement I feel the binding begin
to fray a pale yarn of hairs.
Now I observe strangers praying.
Now I observe strangers pick up
odd pieces of themselves as offerings to me.
Spoken in a dialect that chimes with my own
harmony; they assure me I am not naked
and married to anyone.

Of course they do; there's always
been something of the nun about me, it is
a left over from 'chapel', and later my wish
to take a daily vow of contemplation
interpreted as shunning them.

An Artist Who Knew Adventures

A knock on the door hardly loud
enough to warrant a response.
He had not been expecting visitors.
Hoodie figure facially indeterminate.
Took-a-look as if a portrait
of a dead saint had suddenly
sprung out of the paint
then bursting, as an oiled blister:
"Have you got a moment?"

An artist who knew adventures
he neither invited or wanted.
How cheap the pitch
for such intimate merchandise.
No small savings were worth dipping
into for such an offer of equality.
Our strength is our greatest weakness,
our weakness our greatest strength.
A gap in understanding could have
stolen every moment he ever had.

The Woman With The Neon

The wound spills out trepidation, afraid it
could fester. The mind made up, aware
speaking is a precious gift for
anyone. Wait awhile, weighing words too
heavy to lay down. Resting the case asks
a degree of empathy of all volunteers
who listen.

Blind vision knows in every burden lifted
there's always someone else's toil that
needs to be carried to make up
for handling another person's baggage.
Sharing is a mutual aid society. I'll pick
up yours willingly, please take mine
with you.

And he wasn't sure if it was not simply
easier to carry what he already knew
well, than to take up a share
of an unknown nightmare which he had
not experienced. But then she appeared,
a woman out of the dark to lend him
her light.

Muntjac Deer

Where she went to was never known.
Physically she lived near King's Lynn;
nine months in a hamlet by the Ouse.

"She is like the Muntjac deer.
We see her but she quickly disappears
at the sight of itinerants."

"Ask anyone if they know her and the
answer is always the same.
How can we? For she never stays here,
only long enough to gather dry goods
in her collection of bags."

"It's as if her smile is stoic stiff
with bereavement.
Maybe she lost a part of herself in
some past heatwave; now perpetual
hibernation is upon her and whatever
has gone teases Muntjac like the shades
of shadows in Harding's Pits."

"Rumour has it her home is no more
a house than anywhere else we can
put a finger to; so many empty bowls.
There is no pleasure in them."

"The Huntsman said she used to be
seen reading her own writing from
her outstretched palmed hands
as if she hoped to quote herself."

"I doubt it. What she wrote is rarely
voiced even when answering a question."

And so it was someone once asked her,
"Do you know where you are?"
Her blue eyes lit with what tea lights
she still possessed.
"Yes of course, I am here, here
for the time being."

Then, like the Muntjac deer,
she was gone.

Yellow Canary

You can dance
under the awning and pale drenched light.
All night it has rained elephants and cheetahs
thundering upon a moorland monsoon so deep
in diamonds lacerated bare feet wear ribbons.
Little argument is to be had here.
No need to make an enemy out of anyone.
Brass neck shirt collars turned up offer
faint chance of protection from a stoning.
The bigger the boulder the less reason
to be afraid.

Her hair is sponge blonde with rainwater.
Dyed Rasta locks dance independently
over her eyes.
She has constantly laughed
throughout this crash of hurricanes.
Happy in the hale and thunder, impervious
to the implications of a crisis in the climate.
She rarely reads the small print, spending
the last year in Stockholm watching the way
the people vote with their feet.
Now she jives and sings as a yellow canary,
come to live here permanently because
it will rain every day of her seven lives.

Abergavenny

Stroking the spruce pine and maple
arched body, the old art soundings
found in the dense grain, veins
of music open to the elements.

He had restrung the violin
so it sang like the streams
below the Sugar Loaf.
And he practiced the week away
fiddling arpeggios until his own fingers
had found past paths to a new song.
Those melodies from Bartók, revived,
adding harmonies and restings
where he could simply drone.

Evans had bought the instrument
from a pedlar one Sunday morning
in September last year in Abergavenny.
The old man was passing through
on his way to Cardiff Bay,
selling off his soul because he said
he didn't need it anymore.
"She left me for a winter of silence
and I've no wish to serenade
my own heart."

Cautiously, Evans left the violin
in its case safely stored in the velvet
interior until at long last he began
to barter his charts on footfalls
of percentages.

Who would hear us sing once spring
gave up its gallery to the budding wild?
Who would wish to play poker
with such old notes of love?

Then came an answer
from inside the case, as if spruce were
back on the mountain and the moon
already risen on the bow.
He had spent good money
buying what he needed to know
as a godsend and now all he had
to do was hear it for himself.

Macdeath

Macdeath among the standing stones,
a final resting place in a daily ritual of
remembrance.

Burnt to a crisp scale of skin wrapped
in a bandage of rags. The Black Watch
hands, a white asphalt in this bonfire
tragedy of the Somme in Picardy.
Now they sift cindered soil feeling for
that moment in the smouldering dust
when Macdeath passes by this way.

The two of them hold their ground.
Pulsed feet steaming streams of blood.
Roots reaching down to where the core
of their coming together lies entwined.
Unable to ever part, they dig fingering
a fine fragrance of poppy oil and roses.

Once a warrior signs for their country
Macdeath scribes the names with
certainty, seeking something eternal.
No wars without graves; touch this
ground, feel it move with the presence
of men embalmed in seed. Given time,
less time than imagined, forestry will
return to inhabit Picardy and with it
everything that has not been learnt.

SOLO

solo so slow sooo loow
down double voicing linguistic sound
no language can touch tongue untied
no overdub nodub dubno dubno but
solo in the fish tackle of gargling
larynx out at c see sea wave lo
so   wide
as o
cean
motion surfffffff scho
er ken song
so fast so clipped so stripped of every bit
of acoustic in the chatterbox but not-of
emotion
ecommerce
unedited angles
how deep is the depth of nosong
how high is the falsett o
in each incredulity that breaks from scho
er ken even when below the bottom
of the impossible mouth music echo
no one is so low as to be a lone
but   to the lighthouse we go   to a room
of our own om making   & solo
converse with hannaaaa scho   soul binary

For Hanna Schörken

Libertas

Taking a liberty.
The hope is it remains worth having.
To become visually impaired in plain
sight of the view
is not how it has to be.

No sense in feeling a prisoner.
Such freedoms should
never be in dispute.
All liberties are a bleeding liberty
won, owned by common consent.
This one has been kept hidden.
Taken through the one private
access channel available.
Capture of rapture so precious
when robbing ourselves blind.

A glass-eyed china doll left in an attic
took-or-be-taken, taken-or-be-took,
give-or-be-given, left-or-bereft in
this unexpected cut up intermission.

Why it needed to be so deep
an incision is open to conjecture.
In the event no one dined at the table.
Nor was anyone able to gain exclusive
rights, as god knows they had always
been specific from that day forth.
So unnecessary, calling it a necessity.

The best that can be wished for is to
let liberty be the last bastion of healing.
Allow a shocking consequence become
a final act of forgiving ourselves.

Dove's Anima

In the lea of dove's anima.
Holding the shape of the breast bone,
cupping wings to each shift of breath feels
as if this dove dresses down for the day.
The elderly mother clears this mess
away like a creamed sickness.
Such a lot of soundings rebounding
without any requited flight of fancy.
Fluttering failed promises wrapped round the
palm of piecemeal papers. Peace checked-out,
she held a bird's beautiful body in soft stools.

Remember and recall what those heroic
tales read into Heaney language of epic
lives meant. Flying from the pages, first
saved sayings for evenings when crystal
is polished clean and wide eyes are able
to look into the hour glass
counting a time back for safe speaking.
Whispering the dove's love of letters to
stand out proud of each other.
Pressed into service for echoing Zen
in the way the Tao reverberates finality.
Never loud, but always there in tinnitus.

Now two people cease to hear the
hullabaloo of pigeon-post and internet.
Doves lead quiet lives and will not desert.
Nobody would want to deny an act of love.

And so suddenly it seems there is a need
for anima to address space with signaling.
Let the bird loose, let the dove fly high,
let secreted gentleness have at least height.
What has already passed remains rising above
them. A messenger to nowhere, simply a soul
of a bird seeking to translate to an angel.

An Apocryphal Night

Those who remain tap themselves into an
apocryphal night wrapped in patched rugs
held together by blanket stitch with simile;
lamp lit and the abiding hand of darkness.

Phil in Abergavenny, land of the Pharaohs.
His binocular eyes tracing bird song in the
Bush. Stringing singing into gold leaf lines
he had memorised for the morning's glory.

Darting Julie, balances her clock, calls on
Aretha to pass her the pen and paper she
had carefully put on the table. A reminder
of rhythm. Forwards the notes on Illusion.

At 27, East Bristol, Juniper James changes
a ribbon. Traverses typeface into a script
of spoken-word-mouth-music. In ambient
inherited observation he pauses a beat by

the space bar. Editing out the word in the
ear he designs another mountain in three
lines to those shadows of the disappeared.
What calls the name to this practice genie?

I-do-he-does, of course we do. I write out a
prescription in my scribbled hand. Squeeze
musician meaning from the dead griot who
always loved us. And Julian runs his double

bass against the wall of perfection. Finding
another way for variant voodoo of nymphs
and shepherds to meet Mingus out at 52nd
Street with Stravinsky sharing the *Firebird*.

After we had stolen the saxophone nobody
would talk about it or begin improvising at
the cost of interrupting the hysterical hush
bubbling muted on forked tongue. A night

too long in the making. The saxophone is
not just an object of desire it is a voice of
invocation. This King Super-20 tenor with
pearl keys circa 1958 has been taken into

an enforced retirement by a woodshed of
hoodlums now whispering for fear of the
scale in the dry reed mouthpiece. Around
midnight, too late to request they confess.

Throughout this apocryphal story Peter is
exercising; reconstructing this disfigured
doll making her as exquisite as the violin.
He holds the bow to give her back sound.

Spurn the speech that steals the battered
meanings out of an old testament and let
light come in. The written word of poetry.
Unscrambled syntax cannot be a betrayal.

Introduction To The Well Of Meaning

He began to imagine
The Well Of Meaning
in his head as Georgia drove the old jeep
cross-country grinding the gears around
each covered corner as if daring to meet
a daemon on the other side of the bend.

She spinning the steering wheel in a act
of roulette, he grabbing a line of poetry
to prevent emptying his vomit of nerves
into a flat lap puddle of loose expletives.

Christ did she want to die? Was Georgia
so divorced from the bride that she was
begging the road to decide whether they
remained alive. He tried preserving the
line by challenging it
to repeat every thirty

seconds, inventing a
complimentary verse
in the vain hope *a deep well would ward*
off the inevitable. As the jeep ploughed
into the sheep bursting its belly to guts
through matted fleece
poetry was in the bag.

The Well of Meaning was later dug out
clean from his head, *the survivor in an*
accident costing the price of an animal
sacrificed for the sake of the argument.

The Well Of Meaning

The well of meaning
so divorced from the bride that she was
begging the road to decide
whether they remained alive.
A deep well would ward off the inevitable...
the - well of meaning,
the - survivor in an accident costing
the - price of an animal sacrificed for
the - sake of the argument.

Skewbald

He had shaggy ponies feasting on the field
getting on for a full year. Bought the three
at Hadleigh in exchange for a decently
restored Zephyr with silver trim interior
and an engine without cough or splutter.
The kids had made a fuss of them for a day
or two. Long enough to give them names
and then forget again.

Johnny arrived one morning in October with
a bucket and brush. Nobody knew him from
Adam, just smelt his scent of sweet stable
scrubbing muck off the skewbald because,
"He carrying a herd of parasite on that there
coat, don't deserve to be." The Johnny Boy
sorted the palomino and the bay by midday;
all three gee-gees looking party animals.

At New Year the kids were in Johnny's gang.
Got a sack full of tack from a Romany fella
in Billericay by bartering it for a sheep
they purloined off the Hadleigh marshes;
had no markings to speak of. By February
all three equines were jumping pallets and
oil barrels like it was the Grand National
tote at Becher's Brook.

Johnny The Jockey:
He holds the harness of the horse.
Feels the jog of the jangling bit
and the power in the breath of nostrils

blowing wet across his warm hands.
They will ride fast, gallop the early
morning's furlongs, pull up, unsaddle.
This is not skewbald, this is thoroughbred,
heaving blood and sticky thick sweat
already into new hay mash.

First time they knew of it was the scrap
of postcard and the scruffy snap shot.
Trading-in the palomino for a ticket to
Newmarket to give them the blarney how
he could persuade horses to fly fences like
colliding over a full moon. Johnny the groom
in racing silks, hanging out his washing
on the finishing line.

The painted pony and brood bay mare cover.
A skewbald penis is the length of a fire hose.
Seems like the whole of Hadleigh is standing
around sizing the sex. See it rise up upon the
rear and inject urgency from a sonic boom all
over as fast as folk frolic fiddles. Now go back
to grazing grass before shitting a difference.
They built a dozen houses
on that pony waste ground.

The Footprints

Rather this unspoken than unacknowledged.
Right now neither has any idea where, when
or how commitment is fulfilled, waiting time
is not disclosed nor even what the day looks
like. Whether it be autumn, winter, spring or
summer. Worn rutted tracks read in the dark.
Each day is a lifetime sharing the next steps
until they make paths to place heel and sole
into curvatures of anywhere that creates the
confidence to walk pressing deep footprints.
Nobody runs free without bells and whistles.

Edith

The autumn below the Tor you
were beyond my knowledge of
what's possible. In all things a
light more intense than spring.

The jasmine buds scent white.
Such a heavy fragrance weighs
enough to blister shell of seed
to grow a row of spindly trees.

Edith, we'll never reach that far.
Won't ever go together to such
a place again. We don't see the
other in the patio cyclamen bed.

What I have found is-light-is-lit
by what is earned in earth and
returned back to the sky to fly.
I trust thee for that, dear Edith.

Diamonds In Streams

March 2019 - April 2020

A Spell Of Healing

An expensive practice made solvent
in sleep, there is a healing to be had here,
walking against the wind in the crescendo
of mid-morning mantra,

rough skin of upturned palms smack this map
of cuts and grazes, waterlogged from picking
pink lotus from the pond, beating time out of
the sixteen cycle, panhandling Buddha breath
an expanse of fresh crisp cold air, blown into
the lungs, drawn into the soft low diaphragm
where the healer of Lapis centres the selfless
overlaps of last night's meal of seeds with an
urge to shit and begin the day writing poems

counted out in the dark, blue beads chipped
off an escarpment to decorate a bomb proof
bunker braided between mining fingers and
stubs of old handwriting in the banned book
of the dead; straighten the spine, stretching
vertebrae posture until it lengthens the back
into the barrel of an automatic weapon built
to beggar alms from every secular caliphate
that guards their prayer with blood and guts

spilt onto the floor, wash away yesterday as
if it were unnecessary, as if it were past life
leftovers, as if it were virus, as if it is a blue
stone magic mountain that in reality is only
a spell of healing binding birth and death in

seizures and breath, if torrents of turquoise
drown in the flood then morning must steal
clean bowls from which to eat yourself; raw
meal hunted from the healing of your heart.

Dedicated to Gary Snyder

Plagueground

Today is not quite like any other
they are running a long haul fever
flight to recover their senses
left at the only address
identified as home.

Blue sky morning's weather reporting
broadcast through a bright light of stripes
flagged in slate and shadow;
back where they believe they belong,
dropped into a spring of locked down
potency; no children's games in the
playground, bolted chains at the gate,
this landed land is now
their plagueground;
re-entry arrival running late.

Already the white wood
anemones are open.
Scattered across the rosary
moss and beech cutting below
a dry stone gully. Blackthorn
hedging the edge of hillside
into seclusion.

Walking this path because this path
is not usually used at such a partisan hour.
This path is only known to those in the know
and those in the know will either have visited
earlier or at dusk, after their animals have
been fed, watered and put away behind bars.

For the moment this path is the escape route
out of the house for
a once-a-day-act-of-exercise
with no encounters with neighbours,
or worse, strangers.
Where did these masked people come from?
Possibly a long haul fever flight
to recover their senses close to where they
imagine someone else's handiwork might
help them find their own.

Her Finger Tip

The ground is frayed with frost
laid out by the landscape to
come round to a mush of tinted
light spread out on watering
rust-bleed through an open window.
She writes a shaky signature
into tears of iron with her finger tip.

The night before,
a bottle placed on the bedside table.
Cheap Merlot, no need to waste
the aged Bordeaux, in any case
Argentina red bleeds bitter.
Twisting off the cap took awhile,
taste lacking the strength of guile.

All the time in the world, an empty glass
smudged with face cream finger prints.
The full bottle left to breathe next to two
packets of pills, at hand,
just like time itself, a well-spent sickness.

Now, the present tense is carefully
taken without tablets on the tongue.
One at a time, pricks them out from
the cardboard seal like seedlings
replanted for next season.
Still............
another few months at least.

Picks up the bottle of Merlot,
takes it to the open window sill;
pours the bitter red fluid of slit
blood across the frost and licks
her finger tip.

Lugano

A glorious birthday party,
confidently diving into Lugano
stark naked, the lake surrounding skin
in streams of consciousness
soaking hair suddenly stuck-wet-to-neck.
In water the private part of tits
glistening free of dressing.
Painting points of the elemental
on the tips of pale pink nibbles.

Flattened folds within pictures,
still life in a lit landscape.
Shimmer the background;
shear sheet sunlight
liquid colour controlled to cover the depth
of paper soaking up rivulets of wash.

Wild flowers in a vase,
collected for Friday, no longer wild,
cell-sapping into rainwater.
Push the brush into patterning
red brick and mortar.
Write on the back of fine art
postcards for people given a bowl
of light in water colours.

Dedicated to Winifred Nicholson, artist and painter.
(21st December 1893 - 5th March 1981)

A Far Cry From Eric Dolphy

He and I stand here together.
Two old humanists too much
belief for atheism.
Two old believers too human
for your miracles.

Pursue the length of his lungs
down through the dark tube twist
the cry of our collaboration.

A custodian of the ballad, peeling back
the pages in the library of scores
settled by my pairing poetry.
I catch his wet eloquent breath as if
listening to a far cry from Eric Dolphy.
And though I too turn my autumn leaves
of grass, the very weight of exchange
blots the copy book, singing the sobs
of Blue Note's past as I rob my own
Whitman debt by improvising payment
to his bass clarinet.

    Nothing here impersonates;
    every echo of generosity is
a retold discovery given back to those
storytellers of the dark wood arts
who knew they held the bell and book
in equal measure to be laid down
like everybody will be, in the clay.

But it is a different day,
and I find myself writing these notes
because he blows what he hears me say.
I only needed to be read by the reed.
When listening to Langford this old
humanist believes in the moment.

Lettering Jack

Kerouac pampered his hands
with talcum powder and then wrote
the title out in block capitals.
The letters of the law
cut up in a collage of names
rearranged for a recognition heist.

Call Ace of Spades and call the
whole pack of cards into play.
He punished himself and everybody else
who had supplied his signature to his stack
of providence and configurated the price.

In the colour of her intake of breath
Edie knew it was over for him.
What could she do?
At the end he lit letters to ignite
his Havana cigars.
Created sketches of cinder from
the cremated characters he had
burnt at poker.
Blew smoke rings through Buddhism.
Rolled paper money by scrawling
an unintelligible name in an untraceable act,
licking the black for the Jack of Diamonds
in the final smack on the baize table,
bet a chard watermark against written evidence.
The old cardsharp's loan, paid by an ink cheque
uncorrected in its lettering.

How They Used To Live

A pill box on the hill, this is where
the raincloud and thunder met,
hidden along the lane less
driven; across the steep field dug
into the grass bank like a badger set.

Now it is written that our families
play with fire; babies brought up
with bombshell as headstones.
For each, apiece of peace, given out
as fragile Passover by the Rabbi as
if he were folding my skirts neatly
round my legs for safe keeping
among the past lives sleeping in
Tottenham Court Road underground,
where once upon a time the residue
of warfare hung in the air,
slippery on the steps of the stairs.

She spoke with aplomb, a bomb had
been discovered in the pill box privy,
probably made to measure while
reading *The Way We Live Now.*
In truth she had wiped up so much
mess the polka dots had disappeared
from the table cloth.

When the sun had been put to bed,
Miriam sat down to touch up her
ketchup coloured lips telling fibs
about the long barley growing as
tall as trees, so high Ma built towers
of bread baked for the wake of martyrs.

After the flour feast and Trollope,
Da and Ma dealt in scrap, hiring
fork lift trucks to lift rags to riches.
Writing-off Cortinas, turning them
into sheet metal for hi-jacks.
And as it has been written,
the pill box privy lit up the dawn
like a dose of heavy water.

Anne Sexton's Antenna

The buzz of her sorcery antenna
touches us with a pencil wand
directly where a Pulitzer poem
elects to *Live*, the poet is gone.
Reminding me to safe keep any
scrap of evidence of joie du vie
held in her collection of mycelia.

In this bliss of darkness, a nearly
new year unfolds
out of our waxed ears.
Before six o'clock catches morning,
            the winter owls are calling
to each other through
poltergeist shapes of white maple.
Pipistrelle glide over Silver Street
to be reborn hangmen in waiting.
A surgical blade of laser light lay
warm hands upon her maternity.

I am imaging gambling chess,
playing for pawns down beneath
the predators nest at the side of
rice fields of Thai gold.
She is so happy here, no Bedlam,
no Salem, only this lovely virgin
who never will grow old.

Fortune's blessings for the next
twelve months in Chinatown.
While you, buddy, shelter from the
Shanghai sun. We have our home out
on Mercy Street and are *Her Kind* too.

For NH.

Mere Trinket

Mere trinket hardly worth
the written word, just this
cut diamond crystal taken
from the suede box where
it languished on red velvet
beside a prize china pig.

Mere trinket yet genuine
treasure trove given some
sanctuary within a secret
contraband of his stolen
precious things taken for
the sake of seduction.

Mere trinket of polished
prayer sentenced to spit
a phlegmatic kiss across
verses. Pilgrims caught
pissing onto the napkin,
wet a patch of wisdom.

Bogie In My Head

Be the Bogie in my head that takes
out a death to deny elsewhere.
        I more than anyone I

        have ever met
require the glued up gland
        of humming breath.

If you could advance me
        a Bogie to spit at the wind
and rain I could draw lines on The
        Levels and abandon myself.

        Oh, little grub of currency,
block the host weevil
        that weakens men's nature.

Only a Bogie can bind tiny songs
        like me and stuff this day
        full of poetry sufficient to
relieve me of a need for parables.

Head full of memories turned to
snot-n-god, a pickled fortune of
the future tense, I ask to be ash.

If you could advance me
        a Bogie to spit at the wind
and rain I could draw lines on the
        Levels and recreate myself.

And in that act of affection,
would be just enough St Ives
love to strengthen a storm.

Blow hurricane blow, blow me to
the high mountain top so
I can rest my vertigo and
taste the bit of Bogie I so need.

Unlaid Table

Pass 10.00 and descending in a moan
of weather men, October chants The Fall.
Sitting at an unlaid table with a pen in hand
without note book, no knife, no fork,
no talk, a pause in electricity cut.
The rain outside a low
drone of drenched drumming; sodden thud above
as if the whole eastern seaboard has clapped
thunder across the skies and left the collusion
to split the sense of things.

From Slovenia, by ether, I
had received a fifteen page poem
called *The Creation Of Beauty* about
abandonment.
On first viewing it seemed so naked
and alive, three weeks later each page pulsed.
You tell me Jack, should this really be
The Beauty Of Creation?

I needed to find another layer of clothing.
Began re-reading *Thirteen Moons*,
a story of an almost-child riding across America
to meet the Cherokee.
But I will have to come again to those dark nights
on another day
just as, maybe, Alias who is without
argument, will need to return to me when he
has sorted his fiction from fact
and that could take
a lot more time yet.

Meanwhile, meditate on the big kitchen clock
breathing an out-breath-tock to move the gift
    of verse
so it ticks inside the lighthouse like
    a bright beam at-sea
as I steer pass the rocks
    looking through the window
    into the rose bed pruned
away for winter. An unlaid table
                    has only hard copy.

I Walk This Way With Ease

This morning I walk this way with ease,
servant to myself.
I feel confidence return with breaking
shadows upon an
uneven pavement. See my direction in
and around Bristol's new blind spots.

"Oh, baby, take a trip on me."

This morning I need not check my mirror
before leaving.
I inhabit the body that is beneath me with
light reflections.
The carrier is not burdened with weights.
They were laid bundled against the gate.

What I can do is what I will do, a sufficient
contribution.
I walk this way with ease just as it pleases
me to do so.
My rough sleeper buddies, gone to grass.
I value them as heartfelt, not trappings.

"Don't slip, take a trip on me."

Bad Actors

Rising before dawn was becoming
more difficult.
Like the rehearsal, it takes
time to remember all those lines.
Only so much mind available to any of us.

Memorise the script and write it
down as if this
is a character who waits in
the wings like a new understudy
word perfect and ready to ruin your life.

Bad actors on their best day can go
the short route
to the top simply by keeping
quiet and relying on shutting up.
They mime a white paint roar of thunder.

Place Of Birth

The place of birth was the side of the road,
nowhere she could count on, not an exact spot
to mark her cross for buried treasure.
The wind kept it swept; the rain washed it down.
On her map, birth's swaddling sheets were
hiding in the middle of the fold of the page
tucked into the gap at the compass point.

The detailed encompassing of her own mother's
contractions varies depending on the weather.
The fact is, she was born and eventually
crawled forward and walked-on.
Another sheep sorted, clipped and painted.

A ewe shepherd, certainly.
This woman of perdition's highways
learnt to read the runes of ordnance surveys.
Scratched her initials on the arc of the covenant
and where the river shallows, built a barn above
the flood plain.

In The Saved House (excerpt)

Here in the Saved House
the paintings on the wall are open windows and
offer us views of worlds we can only imagine.
Though our eyes acknowledge
their scenery we remain wedded to this space
they fill; a colour palette of perception,
the distinct size and measurement of their art.

And if here, in our refuge
the old politics have died like old men die then
so be it, there is no room to keep them awake.
In the scheme of parties we are
well shot of their promises. They were lost and
had no house of their own to save the
grubby footprints of their trails through history.

When you come to visit,
please regard this place with some ownership
of your own. Every nesting box is eventually
temporary. When we leave the
spoils gathered over the seasons you can stay
awhile. This door will never close behind
you, unless I'm writing what isn't mine to write.

Eels Gathered In The Bay

Kissed him with confession,
her lips briefly holding forth
good news of another child
he could not remember making in the hay.

He looked at her lips as she
whispered reminders of love,
the circumstances pitched in
song slippery as eels gathered in the bay.

She tasted like salted honey.
Pursed promises of seaweed
soiling their warm earth with
streams of fermentation for another day.

Changing Mirror

The ever present shadow who walked away
decided he did not like this latest change of clothes,
preferred the waistcoat.
Sometimes the rest of us have to pass on what we no
longer recognise. Let him blink each
eye in blurred recognition of the cold shoulder found
in front of the changing mirror.

He addressed feminine, put on the worse
of what they had, the tailored tie and the buttoned
down collar; shaved his
pride of vipers, went off to reside in the Everglade
where the snakes only rattle for the
lonely. He had already run out of songs and was left
listening to a click-backing-track.

After all, an ever present hollow shadow;
who can trail an escape from the debilitating illness?
No witness to sickness.
Better not to go even as far as his house of reptiles.
On the grand scale of zero to infinity
that overwhelming sudden desire to retire gracefully.
On reflection he is transparency.

Roving Over Fantasy

Shysters trading ponies,
the Super-Mare donkeys
in the back of a horse-box.
Up on the hill in a two gallon drum

toasting Bristol Blue glass in lager
and laying bets on Rovers winning
the weekend away.
It was that kind of day with the wind
scrambling for the last of the leaves.

I had been walking from Cumberland Basin,
over the cow bridge, over the A38, over the hill,
worming a waymark into an ascent on Mendip,
before the land takes off for the high skies
and I lose sight of the city, striking out
for the Kingdom of Wrington. I will never get
over Dundry in the way Dundry gets over me.

This a short haul of fly tips and fall-flowers.
The residents on the ridge
cement themselves into place, brick thick
against those broken shacks
and damp bungalows.

This is a survivors colony of pot belly men,
tough women, scraping
tried and tested sufficiency out of
their led intestine guttering guarded by
tied-up barking dogs. Jacks snarl smiles,
taking-me-in as a jerk only passing through.

Garlands grown over the
horseshoe's knuckles in
a box of beauties put out
for the fox to badger a clucking hen.

Below, the Bristol Derby prepares
to criss-cross-cone the streets to
keep visitors at bay.
It was that kind of day, welcoming
the cash but not the inevitable win.

My Alias Critique

This is a precise account:
misplacing the much loved Alias
is not something I would choose
to do lightly, but name-calling myself
is occasionally unavoidably necessary.

Of course, those initials that inscribe
the cardboard cover hold good,
though the fingerprints on the old
keyboard of life are unfortunate.
Alias has a deft hand; clean as a
whistle, flirtatiously playing
Cronin's Hornpipe as if I came from
the Blue Stack Mountains of Donegal.

There had never been any intention
on my part to fall off my stool in school.
In fact the opposite.
I always avoided anywhere too small
for my own head height.
Though scraping the ceiling is rarely
a worry for either of us, falling from
a sturdy chair is another matter.

My Alias has only ever been reserved
for reading reeds.
By definition, I would sooner wash
his mouthpiece than use it to play love songs.

Never offer what you are not prepared to give.
It makes for bad breath and disappointment.
Alias does not carry petitions unless
he is honestly able to swear by them.
Without him I would have carried on paying
the piper to play the tune instead of picking
up a pen and critiquing the melody myself.
(To be exact, it was a track on a black shellac
gramophone I inherited from my daddio.)
I can do this, but I know Alias
is unable to indulge; he who writes what
has previously been read
is far too cavalier for his own roundhead.

It was self inflicted on my part.
In the end we decided to share
our vertigo.
Toppling off a table, sober as judges
grasping each other, pedantically
criticising our reasons for duality.

Anniversaries

Remembering remembrances, not actually
the first occasions. Odd moments when
they grow a wild garden into the foundations
of the brickwork of the brain.
Uneven I could not realise how things would
work out, crooked eventually.

The day Jack Kennedy was shot dead
opposite the grassy knoll I was a Roman
Centurion with a broomstick spear.
Five years later Martin Luther King
was murdered in Memphis.
I am at the kitchen table eating apple pie.
Fifteen months on; a man is on the moon.
They tell me he is Arm Strong, a "hero for our time".
I've no idea what I was doing at that moment
because back then, I didn't care
where anyone was walking.

& so it goes on.
Sunday, Bloody Sunday;
I saw the Bogside Massacre news footage
in black & white on a portable TV in Birmingham.
Played it back, confident in my own innocence.
On the day they took out the Twin
Towering Inferno
I was supposed to be giving evidence
at an adult abuse enquiry, cancelled
because of an axis of evil.

Remembering the facts over fiction, tricks
of memorised meals that *we-don't-make-a*
meal of, licked into shape by slippery tongues
conditioning our taste buds even though
we-don't-make-a song & dance about the news.

The riddle of remembrance, scripted to
occasion like farce; odds & sods signed
off in conspiracy theory; confounding the facts
even when an act is unrelated to the stranger
we continually grow into.
The devil may care, but apparently does not.

& it gets personal.
A child takes her first unaided steps
while I watch the last fifteen minutes
of De Nero in *Heat.*
Now she walks her own talk unaided by actors.
It comes closer.
The Red Super Moon coincides with an anniversary.
A drive back from Wells across the Mendips
the sky suddenly seems to coalesce, celebrating
so special a night as this, with a life lit up in stereo.

Remembering the disturbance of happiness,
a synergy of events. Lines through a climate
of living studiously portray diary data
of notated experiences even though foreign
to what is happening in a faraway country
it might as well be home.

Poetry Drunk Sober

There was a small gang of them,
Khahil Ali, Sam and Dave, Stephen Dix
and Rabbi Jonathan looking like Jerry Garcia
before he went white. Stephen said he always
wrote his poetry drunk sober so as
he could test his solos with notes of replication.

Occasionally the world will turn
on who is in the audience. The Rabbi
could be trusted to applaud and encourage
Sam and Khahil to place their bets on a glass
of cider while Dave sucked rain from
an old water-butt full of spirit vinegar and algae.

The pickling of amber is made for
method players like them. Full of Albion
mantra cut from Queen's English as if each
speech dares to be prophecy and every prayer
their last supper. Breath tested men,
acorns planted among the flowers of the forest.

Whatever badge is worn today will
be thrown away tomorrow. A faded label
from a true friend. Stephen recites his mind
and mouth with all the confidence of the Poor
Law. He mimes Gino Washington
by chancing his dancing to Ms Franklin's *Respect*.

Birthday Blues For A Hip King

In 1957, six years after completing the roll,
Kerouac finally got *On The Road* published.
Hey, Juniper, back then you just sneaked in
for the party.

February 21st 1957 reads like a decent date.
It might as well be then as any other.
Birth comes to those who wait in the womb
and well, baby, that was your day of destiny.
A naked life with fate hanging in the scales,
weighing in words before your time.
I guess you did some kicking and screaming.
Unlike you. How it happens, we are not quite
there to witness. What we become happens
further down the line.

By 1982 Abdullah Ibrahim recorded
Blues For A Hip King.
The following year Bill and I were already playing
our White Boy version, which as far as we were
concerned, sounded as hip-a-lick as we had ever
heard transposed for piano.
So much so we drove midweek to Birmingham
to hear the maestro key the real deal oratorio
to Coltrane in all his blackness and got caught
in the outside lane headlights on our way home.

Today it is raining salt crystal snow
on wet leaves, the motorway is behind you.
I write these good-word-wishes,
knowing most of the stuff that's going down
for you right now.
But you're one hip King and I
know you'll write a way into their sting of
bureaucracy's criminal heist hypocrisy.
Sure, *truth-will-out* over bullshit upon the fire.
But birthdays are brimstone, there will be
more poetry from the hippest King Bee ever to
buzz a rebirth of sentencing.
I write this one for thee.

Selling Spots

The old Lagos trapper had been
selling spots since before he was born.
Cheetah price; swift, smooth
and dollar negotiable
out of the Bush bag straight into a jeep,
no questions about who is who,
you buy we sell, nothing to tell.
Brother Mo, he knows nobody,
only himself: *"But I'm not bought,*
you understand?"

"I am the runt of the litter
and have not the power
to build in brick and stone
or hoist a sagged flag."

In the United Kingdom they flog
blotched spots off the cost of living.
Make a bed here, sleep easy,
no one buys the night.
These are the towers of our strength.
Birthrights sell at bargain prices.
We are pleased you have arrived
to weigh up cost of ethnicity in
our home grown pattern of plain
pure colours.

"I am the prejudice in your
pride, trust me not to
let you down, I can spot a
business opportunity."

Sparrows

Sparrows hopping
in amongst the purple sage,
tearing through a lettuce of the alphabet,
dipping their wings in the water collected
in the chipped ceramic bowl
that used to be the butter dish.

These small brown
birds peck off the odour of
potential predators who hunt them as
a sweetmeat delicacy served upon the
yellow chipped ceramic bowl
that used to be the butter dish.

Sparrows hopping
in amongst the purple sage;
twitch-dance, crumb by crumb, tit bit
by bit, quick to feed off conversation
of potential predators and fly
back into the Mexican Orange.

Quick to feed off
the voices of children happily
tearing through a lettuce of the alphabet
unaware of the hopping sparrows splitting
up every chipped word spilling
back into the Mexican Orange.

My Father's Letter

My father's letter to his '*mother dear*'
was as long and silver as her hair that
grew like wild grass across
her floral patterned aprons.
His paper thin sepia letter gave way
to creases of mapped memory,
swiftly written from Durban,
South Africa in 1945.
A city *"lit up in every window"*
with *"butter on the table."*
"It is how I imagine America could be".
My father's reward for desert fighting,
an opportunity to taste the sugaree.

The lean young men of my generation
only saw what we failed to understand.
My father was my private mystery
until the final years.
Before he died we became close friends.
Our hands met completing jigsaws
precisely laid out on a table in the bay
window with the sun coming in,
shining on our supper. He smiled like
the Mona Lisa and said:
"One day you'll read these letters for free.
I've been unable to talk about killing men
or lick the bitter sweetness in the sugaree."

Oh, Salome

He started life fed as a fair haired foal.
A child of hungry parents who taught
him the catechism on Wednesdays and
starved him on Fridays for-his-own-sake.

He had first danced in Tavistock at the
age of five. Later in Dublin; at eighteen
still green behind the ears he wore the
polka dots in the Brazen Head and sang.

He sang for his sister. Sang like a soul,
slow, with descriptive detail. Now he is
sung-out. He cannot raise his voice off
the twat of the back of his ham tongue.

He feels the pus lying across his chest.
A thick fog of unrung-rayed-worn-wool
pinching the chicken throat in a noose
knot crack inside each encrusted gulp.

He caught long days and nights of this.
The perforated gibbet wrapped around
him; a sheep's shroud covers his groin.
Cramp in the damp flap of the foreskin.

He had willed such a conclusion to come.
Bile begets bile, swearing his theology is
but ballet's belief in baptism; a phantom
renewal creates its own rock face crevice.

He wore the repertoire as an old existence.
Now he must choke on every choice word
he had ever spoken. Such a priest as this
could have had a second chance to dance.

Oh, Salome, whose face is in that old thick
head on the platter left here to be mocked
by the dyed blonde mothers of men? Yes,
he became a woman but then cursed them.

Rough Diamonds

Six Famous American men

(i)

The bass line to *Goodbye Pork Pie Hat*
feels as slinky as a walk in the park
when it breaks into dancing on the grass.
Pass the 'Keep Off' sign, pitched below
the bottom and holding the hands that
pluck the strings which cut into the wires
of a retro Roberts radio slightly off signal.

"My name is Charles if you don't mind,
save your Charlie's for the silent movies.
I got plenty of top out of the Lion's Head.
Roars, count-me-inter-three."

And the hip accent that unwrapped
Fables Of Faubus still skips
it's recorded beat into "Ohhhhhh, Lord......"
haranguing the white supremacist
Governor of Little Rock, Arkansas
seventy years after the fact
with a further seventy to go.
Faubus is going down in history
as the guy who tried to stop black kids
registering for school.... "Ohhhhhhhhh, Lord!"

The Black Saint at the White House
weeping whispers to a Salt Peanuts President:
"Me, myself, I, ain't what we seem to be."
Finally, quite still, squeezed paralysed
into a wheelchair; you can just wheel him
right out of Whitie, go get him his private cab.
Wanna know a great life lived? Hear it here.
In the middle of Dannie and the Underdog
smacking at the bass 'n' traps.

(ii)

America singing in its sleep; a dream of dalliance
with nature naked, a union of their own
rough diamonds panned for gold beyond
the grass prairies. Loving the sons and daughters
of the body electric holding erect power
through the gift of greening their poet of
the bivouac. America, what do we see and hear in
your *strong melodious songs* that could
bring you back to earth, to the beauty of
your independence and a grounding of Columbus?
Long ago, in the unique history you so seek,
in the opening of his eyes, you had a softly
spoken poet who surprised our ears with loving.

(iii)

I got my Captain Beefheart badge
and a genuine Obama T-shirt bought with
redundancy money.
I managed to find a copy of Lenny Bruce's
book before it went through the roof when
he was still at large.
Of course Steve Jobs,
but he was a strange deaf soldier and I didn't
like his terminology.
I got Captain America to the point I
can do without him.
American Psycho, The Deerhunter
and the whole of the first series
of Spacey in House of Cards,
now discarded for obvious reasons.

But I can't get pass Bill's gates even when
they are left wide open.
He's far too tech expensive,
beyond my charity and comprehension.
So truly philanthropic it's getting
tricky debating wealth distribution.
But I found I could not write this poem
without him or at least not in the manner
that I write poetry.

(iv)

Xeroxed outta sight
Andy, Andy, Andy, Andy
took me to the 'lectric chair.
Pitched charred execution black.
Only shades of ashes sitting there.

(v)

I don't know what you do with war heroes.
Get the heroic description correct I guess.
Do my best to enunciate meaning explicitly.
Write reality and let each reader do the rest.

Vietnam was no contest, bloodiest of bad
and hero is as hero isn't. On the other hand
what we make of valour is recognise a man
measured in the breadth of guts in conflict.

A burning jet on a stricken aircraft carrier.
Escapes, saves another man as he does so.
Later, captured, imprisoned, tortured, and
contextually it all adds up to Johnny Hero.

In the mathematics of politics delete the
arguments on arguments; what's in name
and number. A rotten resurrection will try
to cast a Senate side of The Great Divide.

(vi)

Nobody's Negro.
The word nor the humanity is for sale.
A written civility of rights
belongs to no one other than the reader
and the author scratching lone exile
into notebooks of habitations.
Typeface talking blackface recalling story
after story onto the creased white paper
spilling across the wooden floor like litter.

Whoever has the key to *Giovanni's Room*
can stay there.
Whoever has the match to *The Fire Next Time*
can strike it once.
Whoever climbs the high crevice will
Go Tell It On The Mountain.
Whispering in their buddies ears
about the beat of *Jimmy's Blues*
and how it's possible to refuse to be typecast.

Thumbprint

Today there would be no need to construct
another placard and walk the streets.
The women stood in line thumbing a vote.
They took their place in the queue
and waited to receive permission to print
identity by taking the matter in hand
and deciding the fate of men.
She pressed her thumb upon the paper
with all the deliberation of an artist.
It had to be a clear mark. True to herself.
After all, this would be proof
of a small piece of power.
Today she would be counted, given
a silent voice with her thumb.

SUPER
RANCI

The Blue Horn

Picture this painted protagonist,
no need to know his hash-tag.
Neither did he, not with any certainty.

But a musician knows a saxophone
backwards; you can hear its beauty
by the way he holds it in his hands.
Hugging the blue horn to his chest.
How a young father cradles his kin.

He blew lines through beaten metal,
pitching and extending the pulse of
the undulating underbelly through a
soft oesophagus into throat and air.
Yet he stands sprayed into a corner.
Staring out of a wall that cut him at
the top of his head and flecks his
face with pitted paint.

The marks of this man speak to me
with all the same precise pressure
pressed upon the razor blade shaving
sound into his reed.
He visibly appears in a swift and salty
stroke of a shaken aerosol-can playing
a riff in the unheard audacious ballad
smeared through the stencil and left
to weather with the printed word.

A musician not acknowledged
because all ears are listening for the
next best thing unaware he has
already graced a note by blowing up
graffiti in blue.

The International

In our broken English we became
The International.
A blended nation made foreign
by a distinct turn of phrase.
Our skin colours shading hereditary.
The weight of wording heavy
on the vine of the collective tongues
slapping at French shrugs,
interrupting in Italian and finding
the course of history parked
in Berlin long after The Wall
has ceased to be a tourist attraction
for lovers of spy fiction facts.

That uncertain age, marking me
a marked man with
a perchance to speak before
he is spoken to. A bandit
with a wallet of Euro notes rubbing
against sterling, money turned
rotten by intent. An exit made mine
and tomorrow we will kid
ourselves we know a better way.
That history will judge us
with a deeper pocket than
we extend to the beating rhythms
of last night's insolvency.

The climate here has heated far
too quickly for these
suited occupants of Davos.
They did not see Maria's
sister sharing a plastic water carrier
with the family at the Hungarian
border having given their girls away.
Of course we British bargain
elsewhere in the world. Pick up
our international reputation
through offshore limitations
by offering the hand of friendship
to anyone paying in dollars.

The Bread Of Heaven

All afternoon they spread dripping
on the bread of heaven.
Raised their voices in choral waves
of Welsh independence,
thick in buttered daffodils milking
the air with the songs of
their fathers and leaving a woman
to wash up their words.

This scattering of toasted crumbs
are given to the birds as
tasty peace offerings to be pecked
over and translated into
Thomas onto Thomas by Thomas.
And may Gwen John be
afforded the fame of her portraits
rather than baking a loaf.

A Week In Mozambique

"We are Africans, we have the genesis
of civilisation buried in our bodies.
You've heard it chanted in a dozen
different dialects fragrant with Latin.
In the shanties we're not difficult to dress up,
clothed in ochre pounding maize and millet,
swigging Coca Cola straight from the crate.
Yeah, sell our plastic crucifix for bags of beans.
We've no tears to spare for a stage of graves.
The molecular makeup of Mozambique
is our pride and misery.
Go home and tell them what they wanna hear.
We Africans gave ground to your slavery,
in return received aid and Aids."

I was born white in the East End
on a Thursday in 1952.
Loved and lucky, delivered by being golden.
Knock on my door with nothing; every existence
imposes the requirement to save for our old age.
I left Sonny planting saplings in a cemetery.
He had plans to "grow a forest", though he
looked like a man digging a hole for himself.
For sure, I spent a week in Mozambique only
carrying what it cost in one small case and my
conscience; even case and conscience were
poor pickings compared to the mineral wealth
that got no further than the lining of pockets.
Bilal spent the best part of his days translating
for me and was sick of it.

There is no point hanging myself out to dry.
I came through Calvary without a second glance.
No chance, they had no chance;
Bilal was dead before I even reached home.

Coward

I am a man
still scared of heights
if cornered in a place not of my own choosing.
I am a man
given sand in my salary
for fearing to face the reality of my decisions.

I am a man
paddling in unsalted sea,
lost on the edge of oceans I am forever losing.
I am a man
frightened to dive for pearls
because I crawl through water as if it is desert.

I am a man
wondering why heroism
continually punches my wound with bruising.
I am a man
asking for salvation
when I know the cost is more than it is worth.

I am that coward
who ran away at the start.
I am the name the coward
tattooed across his heart.
I acknowledge the coward
will swim through the tidal wave.
I cannot praise the coward
when he wins and call him brave.

Bristolians

That summer,
she lay her tilted head
in the depth of white cotton pillows,
her silver strands of hair patterning
the look of sleep as if these tresses
inadvertently creased the fabric.
When she closed her daylight eyes
they stroked the pale skin's lining.

She and the man were old friends
and that was the half of it.
But he regularly stole these
morning moments to gaze again;
she was forever a young girl.
So delicate her breathing, so much width
in the wisp of life living in her sleep.
He shivered. Like Josef.
There is no deception
even in the warmth of watching her.
The way this so finely lined mouth
momentarily trembled in her top lip,
squeezed into the thickened breath
of thinking dreams.

When she wakes
it is never immediate.
Like a coming-to
of dawn unfolding discreetly,
paling moon without the eye
seeking the exact second
dreams fall from view.

Firebrand

All the firebrand of nature
wrapped in a blanket of hemp.
Hair pickled with soft scent of Chew
bottom bed where the runoff trickle
crosses the stone and Jersey cattle
milk the grass of greenery.

He told me his body had
been there bivouacked under
blackthorn for two days, he intended
to stay another two then head east to
Wiltshire to take cover on the range.
"Bedstraw scrub and scratch."

His voice slow and silted,
gathering grit in the crevices
of gut, a faint hint of open country
far away. "Ausstraalia" receives the
songlines to an immigrant's icon.
"I grow in my own carcass."

Later I returned bringing
some stuff he probably did not
need and found he had already gone.
Packed away home to go hide among
a regiment of midges itching for his
skin on a chaff of chalklands.

Sung Mass

Devils and demons
have branded our birthmarks.
Do not seek to see them
they never show their faces.
Now they are silent
and await your invitation.
Let Shiva be defined by
the name that you call him.

Spell out your symbol
and sing self a sleep-song.
Practice those voices
left for us to hear here.
As they fall silent
like night fell to darkness
let Shiva be your witness
to those names remembered.

Two Shorts

Rōshi Koan

Rōshi, you have travelled by aeroplane
from the other side of the world
to guide us in the way of the Buddha,
what question should I ask?

Walking my return I will consider my answer.

Poem 111

He says he
is sure that if we ever convince him
          he will come back for more.

(Instead of 'convince', the reader can use any verb of their choosing. In doing so they will not alter the intended meaning.)

Lightning Source UK Ltd.
Milton Keynes UK
UKHW020917180122
397328UK00006B/127

9 781839 758508